The Chartered Institute of Management Accountants

CIMA

Management Accounting and Strategic Human Resource Management

John Innes
University of Dundee, UK

Reza Kouhy
University of Dundee, UK

Rishma Vedd
University College of the Cariboo, Canada

This publication arises from the research project 'Management Accounting and Strategic Human Resource Management' which was funded with a research grant from the CIMA Research Foundation. The award of a Research Foundation grant, and the publication of findings in this format, indicates that the recipient has successfully passed two separate peer review processes, which also involved practitioner assessors. The views expressed in this publication are the authors' own, and do not necessarily represent those of CIMA.

Acknowledgements

The authors wish to thank the Research Foundation of the Chartered Institute of Management Accountants (CIMA) for funding the research on which this report is based, and Rebecca Burrows of CIMA for her encouragement and administrative assistance. We wish to thank all the managers and accountants who gave generously of their time and knowledge in helping us to prepare the four case studies contained in this report. Without their assistance this research project would not have been possible. We dedicate this report to all our interviewees.

First published in 2001 by:
The Chartered Institute of Management Accountants
63 Portland Place
London
W1B 1AB

ISBN 1 85971 486 2

Printed in Great Britain

Contents

Abbreviations

CEO	Chief Executive Officer
CPC	Canada Post Corporation
CPSI	Customer Perception Satisfaction Index
CSI	Customer Satisfaction Index
EOS	Employee Opinion Survey
ER	Employee relations
ESI	Employee Satisfaction Index
FTE	Full-time equivalent
HR	Human resource
HRM	Human resource management
HRPDP	Human Resource Planning and Development Program
IR	Industrial relations
MA	Management accounting
MEC	Management Executive Committee
MOSDP	Mail Operations Supervisory Development Programme
PDV	Purpose, direction and values
R&D	Research and development
RIR	Recordable incident rate
RM	Royal Mail
RMEC	Royal Mail Executive Committee
RONA	Return on net assets
Sc&NI	Scotland and Northern Ireland (division of Royal Mail)
SHQ	Strategic Headquarters
SHRM	Strategic human resource management
SMA	Strategic management accounting
WLE	Weycan Leadership Education
WSI	Work Systems Improvement

Executive Summary

This research project investigated the role of management accounting (MA) in relation to strategic human resource management (SHRM). Questionnaire surveys in the UK and Canada revealed that management accountants provide much information for decision-making, setting targets and performance measurement in the SHRM process (Kouhy and Vedd, 2000).

The questionnaire surveys also helped to identify leading-edge companies for four in-depth case studies conducted using a grounded theory approach. In the Royal Mail (Scotland and Northern Ireland) case, the human resource (HR) strategies included employee flexibility, leadership and training and development. At the strategic headquarters level management accountants provide information and analyse HR strategies to aid decision-making. At the divisional level management accountants are members of the focus groups which help to develop HR strategies and a management accountant is a key member of the divisional executive committee which decides and monitors HR strategies. At the divisional level management accountants provide information for (a) planning and implementing HR strategies (such as reducing the number of temporary employees and increasing the number of permanent employees to improve customer service); (b) measuring performance of HR strategies (such as training and development); and (c) reporting on HR strategies.

In the Canada Post case, the HR strategies included human resource planning and development programme, leadership profile, teamwork and employee recognition. A management accountant is a member of the most senior management group involved in strategic decision-making. Management accountants provide information for decision-making (such as workforce management), setting targets (such as employee training and development), controlling cost, performance measurement (such as a compensation plan for sales personnel) and benchmarking against other organisations. In addition management accountants are working with the HR group to develop an HR scorecard.

In the TDG case the HR strategies included 'Investors in People' (a government-sponsored programme), training and development (including management skills), drivers' training and communication, and safety at work. A management accountant is a member of the management committee recommending HR policies. Management accountants review the costs and effectiveness of the salary scheme and the training programme and monitor accident records. Management accountants are also involved in providing information for issues such as redundancy pay, loyalty payments, placement costs and decisions such as whether to work overtime or hire agency employees.

In the Weycan case, the HR strategies included health and safety, competitive leadership development, work systems improvement and diversity of employees. At headquarters a management accountant is a member of the executive committee deciding HR areas of emphasis. At the divisional level management accountants play a role in analysing the reasons and costs of accidents and providing suggestions for improvements. Management accountants provide information about the profit implications of employee training and specifically about competitive leadership development. Information on the non-financial performance measures on the health and safety strategy is provided by management accountants.

In summary, these four case studies show that management accountants contribute in many different ways to SHRM such as:

- providing information for SHRM planning;
- analysing HR strategies;
- providing information for HR decision-making;
- measuring HR performance (financial and non-financial);
- benchmarking;
- reporting HR performance.

In all four case studies HR managers would like management accountants in the future to provide even more assistance, particularly by providing more information for developing and setting SHRM targets, measuring human resource management performance (financial and non-financial) and SHRM decision-making. Human resource managers would also prefer to see management accountants in future having a wider business knowledge and being more of a business partner. However, the results of this research project show that management accountants can and do contribute to the SHRM process.

1 Introduction

1.1 Objectives

This research project explores the current role of management accounting (MA) in relation to the strategic human resource management (SHRM) process. The two main objectives are to find out:

1. The existing MA information provided within the context of the SHRM process.
2. Managers' and accountants' views on what role MA information could play in SHRM in the future.

In recent years there has been a debate about the 'new' role of MA (e.g. Bromwich and Bhimani, 1994). Traditional management systems rely on financial measures that may reveal little about progress in achieving long-term strategic objectives. More recently, MA has begun to focus on planning and strategic decision-making (Simon, 1992). Management accounting has an important role to play in providing efficient and effective information to contribute to the success of the strategic management process (Vilgoen, 1994).

Similarly, the field of human resource management (HRM) has been integrated into the strategic management process, developing a new discipline referred to as SHRM (Wright and McMahan, 1992). In this highly competitive environment, organisations are searching for strategies to provide competitive advantage. In this search, attention is now turning to human resource (HR) strategy. By utilising more effectively their human resources, organisations can enhance their competitiveness. Armstrong (1995) suggests that, in order to improve performance, HRM must be able to understand the language of MA. Strategic human resource management is being increasingly recognised as one critical component of any organisation's strategy where the expanded role of MA could play a key business partnership role. There is recognition that MA information is of vital importance to management decision-making to ensure the success and survival of organisations in a competitive environment.

An organisation's strengths are based on its resources, and one of those strengths is a highly skilled workforce. This highly skilled workforce can become the cornerstone of its strategy and the basis on which to build competitive advantage. Therefore, the focus of this research project is the contribution made by MA within the context of the strategy involving human resources by which the organisation intends to achieve its objectives and carry out its intended mission.

There is a shortage of empirical evidence that can be used to provide comprehensive descriptions of the practice of MA in relation to SHRM. This raises the questions, 'Currently, what is the role of MA?' in the context of SHRM and, from a managerial perspective, 'What could be the role of MA in future?' The study explores the current role of MA in relation to SHRM, which is an area of great importance and significance to managers in gaining competitive advantage.

1.2 Overview

A literature review of the phenomenon under study, that is, strategic management accounting (SMA) and SHRM, is presented in Chapter 2. Based on this review, a questionnaire was developed (e.g. Schuler and Jackson, 1987; Lengnick-Hall and Lengnick-Hall, 1988; Guest, 1990; Hendry and Pettigrew, 1990; Riahi-Belkaoui, 1992; Pfeffer, 1994).

The analysis of the questionnaire surveys of 500 UK companies and 500 Canadian companies provided further knowledge to explore the issues relating to the role of MA in relation to SHRM. The main findings of these two questionnaire surveys were:

1. The current contribution of MA information in the SHRM process is relatively low but higher in measuring performance, providing information on performance indicators and on productivity.
2. Management accountants are less involved in developing HR strategy but are more involved in evaluating and controlling HR strategy.
3. Human resource managers would like to see management accountants taking a more proactive role.

Most detailed results from the questionnaire survey can be found in Kouhy and Vedd (2000). The survey also provided a basis for identifying suitable companies for the case study stage of the research. The four in-depth case studies (two UK companies and two Canadian companies) are detailed in Chapters 3–6, and the conclusions from this research project are given in Chapter 7.

2

Literature Review

2.1 Management accounting

Historically, MA was grounded in factory accounting and cost accounting. Management accounting was simply involved in the mechanics of recording, tracing and assigning costs rooted in past data (Anthony, 1989). During the 1980s, new challenges emerged for MA and the traditional roles and methods were challenged. Organisations discovered new manufacturing technologies. In the new environment, many companies found that their traditional cost accounting measures were inhibiting the introduction of innovative manufacturing processes and technologies. Since the 1980s, academics and companies have been developing new management accounting procedures to meet the challenges of rapidly changing technologies, a shift in emphasis from manufacturing to information services, an increase in the number of mergers and acquisitions, and a move towards deregulation, privatisation, downsizing and vigorous global competition.

The traditional management systems that rely on financial measures reveal little about the changing environment. More recently, Shank and Govindarajan (1993) explain that MA has traditionally had an *internal* focus as well as a *narrow value-added* perspective. Criticisms of traditional MA methods were also made (e.g. Johnson and Kaplan, 1987). A series of papers criticised MA for not keeping up with the changes in manufacturing technology (Kaplan, 1983, 1984, 1988). Another element of Kaplan's critique is the heavy emphasis placed on financial accounting by MA. He further argues that much of the research on MA is not relevant to actual MA practice. In addition, Berliner and Brimson (1988) criticise the role of traditional MA for a failure to achieve more organisational goals.

The changing role of MA is concerned with the future and meeting organsational goals by working with the management team to influence manager behaviour to have a positive impact on decision-making (Anthony, 1989). Today's MA systems must be designed to support the above trends. The challenge for management accountants is to add value constantly as part of the management team, while innovating and acquiring the skills and knowledge to be competitive (Birkett, 1995). Therefore, the shift in the role of management accountants is from a traditionally heavy reliance on financial data to reflect a more creative role in the pursuit of competitive MA, thereby providing information that creates value. For this to take place, management accountants possibly need to take a broad *value-added* or *value-creation* perspective by exploiting all the linkages among the elements in the value chain (Shank and Govindarajan, 1993).

Bromwich and Bhimani (1989) suggest that for management accountants to play a major role in the twenty-first century, 'they must lead in the further growth of successful innovations, continue to experiment, to seek out new ways of using their existing expertise, and to enlarge their competence by seeing management accounting as a much broader function' (p.6). Furthermore, Bromwich and Bhimani (1989) present their discussion on the continued development of management accounting as being more outward looking and emphasised a '*strategic*' approach – strategic management accounting (SMA).

2.2 Strategic management accounting

Roslender et al. (1998) provide a brief overview of the developments of MA, with an emphasis on strategic management. They suggest that there is a need for a measure of 'strategic' MA information for professional groups within the business organisation and:

> If it wished to remain an important function in the business organisation, management accounting had to become more *strategically* [our emphasis] orientated. Continuing to furnish mainly traditional, essential internal information, whatever its merits, was unlikely to serve the profession well in the future. (p.46)

Management accounting has begun to focus on planning and strategic decision-making (Simon, 1992). A study by Ittner and Larcker (1997) indicates that organisations are placing greater emphasis on MA involvement in their strategic planning process where:

> Management accountants are increasingly being called upon to take an active role in providing information for strategic decision-making and monitoring the implementation and success of strategic plans. (p.310)

Management accounting has an important role to play in providing efficient and effective information to contribute to the success of the strategic management process (Vilgoen, 1994). The MA contribution in the strategic planning process may, for example, provide detailed analysis of the organisation's major programmes to implement its strategies, monitor ongoing performance and provide suggestions for corrective measurements to compete successfully and increase profitability and market share.

Thus, the challenge for management accountants is to support the entire management process of planning and controlling all aspects of both operational and strategic activities to be competitive. Simmonds (1981) used the term 'strategic management accounting' for the expanded role of MA in providing information in assisting strategic decision-making. He defines SMA as:

> The provision and analysis of management accounting data about a business and its competitors for use in developing and monitoring the business strategy, particularly relative levels and trends in real costs and prices, volume, market share, cash flow and the proportion demanded of a firm's total resources. (p.26)

According to Bromwich and Bhimani (1994), the role of MA is not to take over the role of strategy formulation but rather to be an active player providing the information required in planning and controlling the strategy of the business. They also point out that MA plays a key role in 'target costing' – the setting of cost targets for each stage of a product's life cycle. For an organisation to achieve its strategic goals, the contribution of information from all the disciplines must be integrated. In defining the role of MA, researchers (e.g. Riahi-Belkaoui, 1992; Ward, 1992) suggest an expanded role for MA from its limited scope of cost accounting to a multi-disciplinary integrated field aimed at assisting management in strategic decision-making. Strategic management focuses on integrating, marketing, finance/accounting, production/operations, HR and R&D aspects of a business to be successful.

Ward (1992) refers to SMA as accounting for strategic management where strategic management is an integrated management approach that draws together all the individual elements involved in planning, implementing and controlling business strategy. Thus, SMA provides information for decision-making and also information about alternative business strategies.

The position of SMA has been perceived as being at the nerve centre of all information and data flows within the entire organisation. Management accounting is all about supplying the right information to the right people at the right time, and this can be expressed in the context of the business strategy and the strategic plan (Ward, 1992). Management accounting has an important role to play in providing efficient and effective information to contribute to the success of the strategic management process (Vilgoen, 1994). The success of the strategy is in the information provided by MA throughout the strategic management process (Caillouet and Lapeyre, 1992).

One of the most important and vital parts of the strategic management process is performance measurement, and this was one of the most challenging areas for practitioners and researchers in the 1990s. According to Grady (1991), performance measures are linked to organisational strategy. Strategy without performance measurements is strategy without objectives. Thus, performance measures are derived from strategy and emerge to support business objectives and therefore provide all management levels with feedback on how well the strategies and objectives are being met. This enables management to identify, correct and promote continuous improvement. It also provides competitive benchmarking information in developing competitive position. According to Berliner and Brimson (1988):

> A key factor in ensuring the successful implementation of a company's strategic plan is performance measurement, which measures business and plant performance in relation to the goals and objectives developed in the planning process; provides timely information for identifying and eliminating activities that add no value; and provides timely information on causal factors that may lead to manufacturing improvements. (p.159)

Performance measurement is an integral part of the strategic process where SMA plays a vital role in providing performance indicators, in making strategic decisions and in implementing a performance measurement system (Grady, 1991). For the control system to be effective it should be related to the organisational strategy, incorporate all the steps in the control process, blend both objective and subjective performance measures, provide feedback in a timely fashion, and be accepted by members of the organisation. Miles and Snow (1978) argue that an organisation's control system should link to its strategy in order to ensure that the firm's activities are unified with its strategy. Additionally, the work of Simons (1990) focuses on management control systems that articulate with the strategic management process and are important in both the formulation and the implementation stages. In his model, Simons introduces new concepts to link the management control system with competitive advantage and also illustrates how 'top managers use formal systems to guide the emergence of new strategies and ensure continuing competitive advantage' (p.127). External environmental information is critical in providing analysis during formulation of the strategic planning process, and Clarke (1995) identifies the drive of SMA as being 'to provide information concerning the firm's market and its competitors, and to focus on internal data from a strategic perspective' (p.47).

Bromwich and Bhimani (1989) suggest that for management accountants to play a major role in the twenty-first century, 'they must lead in the further growth of successful innovations, continue to experiment, to seek out new ways of using their existing expertise, and to enlarge their competence by seeing management accounting as a much broader function' (p.6). Many models of strategic planning assume that strategy formulation and strategy implementation are distinct, separable activities, and posit that strategy formulation initiates strategy development (Mintzberg, 1990). Alternatively, other researchers (e.g. Mintzberg and Waters, 1985) hold that strategy formulation and implementation are not separable, that is, 'thinking cannot be separated from doing'. Collier and Gregory (1995) also suggest that SMA is becoming an integral part in providing information in decision-making.

Roslender et al. (1998) consider the interface of MA with disciplines such as marketing and suggest that 'strategic management accounting is claimed to release MA from the factory floor, thereby allowing it to aid directly in meeting new market challenges' (p.45).

Therefore, there is growing evidence of SMA activities being pursued in an interdisciplinary manner. The challenge for this research project is to identify the role of SMA in relation to the discipline of SHRM. For organisational strategy to be effective, SMA information needs to be integrated in the strategic management process.

2.3 Strategic human resource management

Bratton (1994) defines SHRM as:

> that part of the management process that specialises in the management of people in work organisations. HRM emphasises that employees are the primary

> resource for gaining sustainable competitive advantage, that human resources activities need to be integrated with the corporate strategy, and that human resource specialists help organisational controllers to meet both efficiency and equity objectives. (p.5)

SHRM is an approach to the overall direction the organisation wishes to pursue in achieving its objectives for creating and sustaining competitive advantage through people. The key element in SHRM is that HR strategies are integrated with corporate strategies in order to gain sustainable competitive advantage. Integration is where HR policies coincide with one another as well as with other areas of policy such as marketing, production and finance. Therefore, SHRM is regarded as an overall approach to deal with issues such as ensuring that the organisation has the people it needs, along with training, motivation, reward, flexibility and teamwork, all of which facilitate the successful achievement of the corporate strategy.

Some researchers focus on human resource management (HRM) as strategic integration (Schuler and Jackson, 1987; Lengnick-Hall and Lengnick-Hall, 1988; Hendry and Pettigrew, 1990; Wright and McMahan, 1992). Hendry and Pettigrew (1986, p.21) suggest the main features of SHRM as:

- the use of planning;
- a coherent approach to the design and management of personnel systems based on an employment policy and manpower strategy, often underpinned by a philosophy;
- matching HRM activities and policies to some explicit business strategy;
- seeing the people of the organisation as a 'strategic resource' for achieving 'competitive advantage'.

Hendry and Pettigrew (1990, p.35) further state that 'we see HRM as a perspective on employment systems, characterised by their closer alignment with business strategy'. Guest (1989) suggests that SHRM is largely about integration. According to Guest (1990), the driving force behind SHRM is the pursuit of competitive advantage in the marketplace through provision of high-quality goods and services, through competitive pricing linked to high productivity, and through the capacity to swiftly innovate and manage changes in the organisation in response to changes in the marketplace.

Storey (1987) points out that SHRM has its 'hard' and 'soft' dimensions. The hard dimension looks to the integration of HR policies with business strategy, resulting in a competitive advantage. It emphasises 'the quantitative, calculative, and business strategic aspects of managing the headcount resource in as "rational" a way as for any other economic factor' (p.6). According to Legge (1995), the hard model reflects a 'utilitarian instrumentalism'. Hard SHRM strategies are concerned with improving utilisation of employees, by means of a cost-effective approach, and their focus is ultimately human *resource management*. Legge (1995) defines the soft dimension as the 'developmental humanism' model and, while still emphasising the importance of integrating HR policies with business objectives, sees this as 'the treatment of employees as valued assets, a source of competitive advantage through their commitment, adaptability, and high quality' (p.66).

A business strategy requiring high quality and greater customer responsiveness might achieve its objective by adopting a soft SHRM policy that seeks to generate greater employee flexibility and commitment. The soft version emphasises communication, motivation, commitment and leadership. For example, open communication with employees about organisational strategies tends to gain commitment by employees towards achieving organisational objectives. The emphasis is therefore on generating commitment via 'communication, motivation and leadership' (Storey, 1987, p.6). The results from a study by Truss et al. (1997) found that 'no single organisation adopted either a pure soft or hard approach to human resource management' (p.69), and the credibility of HRM will continue to remain a problem as a result of inconsistency between hard and soft HRM (Vaughan, 1994).

2.4 Strategic human resource management and competitive advantage

Historically, organisations have competed through technological innovation, the availability of capital and access to markets, but organisations must now use their people to achieve a competitive edge and take a serious look at how their HR policies and practices are contributing to the total business strategy (Lawler, 1992).

Lado and Wilson (1994) suggest that 'the resource-based view can contribute to sustained competitive advantage through facilitating the development of competencies' (p.699). Barney (1991) proposes that, in order to generate competitive advantage, an organisation's resources must be valuable, rare, non-substitutable and not be easily copied. Wright and McMahan (1992), in their conceptual model of theoretical frameworks for studying SHRM, attempt to focus on HRM practices to generate competitive advantage. According to them, 'the resource-based view of the firm focuses primarily on the relationships among strategy, HR practices, and the HR capital pool, and the behavioural approach is primarily concerned with how strategy, HR practices and HR behaviours are interrelated' (p. 299).

Human resource management policies and practices create resources and competencies (firm specific skills) which are difficult to imitate. These resources contribute to competitive advantage. Hendry and Pettigrew (1986) argue that:

> HRM [has] a role in creating competitive advantage, in which the skills and motivation of a company's people and the way they are deployed can be a major source of competitive advantage. A company can methodically identify wherein its human resource strengths lie and gear its HRM policies and business strategies towards utilising and developing these advantages. The HR skills that will be crucial for the future in its industry can be identified, and it can take steps to acquire this. (p.6)

Schuler and Macmillan (1984) provide case examples of 20 companies that successfully pursued two specific thrusts – cost/efficiency or product differentiation – using HRM practices to achieve competitive advantage. They then illustrate how HR planning, staffing, appraising, compensating, training and development, and union–managerial relations were directed towards achieving the cost/efficiency or product differentiation strategic objectives.

Lengnick-Hall and Lengnick-Hall (1988) suggest that the achievement of competitive advantage through people requires that HR activities be managed from a strategic perspective. In the 1990s, the link and relationship between effective HRM, firm performance and competitive advantage of organisations have been the subject of enquiry and is one of the most challenging areas for practitioners and researchers (Arthur, 1994; Dyer and Reeves, 1995; Kochan and Dyer, 1995; Kamoche, 1996). For example, Kamoche (1996, p.213) suggests that, 'the strategic human resource management literature is increasingly concerned with whether human resources can be a source of competitive advantage'. In addition, there are writers, such as Schuler and Macmillan (1984) and Porter (1985), who agree that HR management can help to create a source of sustained competitive advantage. Pfeffer (1994) concludes that:

> Achieving competitive success through people involves fundamentally altering how we think about the workforce and employment relationship. It means achieving success by working with people, not by replacing them or limiting the scope of their activities. It entails seeing the workforce as a source of strategic advantage, not just as a cost to be minimized or avoided. Firms that take this different perspective are often able to successfully outmanoeuvre and outperform their rivals. (p.16)

2.5 Strategic human resource management and organisational performance

Arthur (1994), Huselid (1995) and Ichniowski et al. (1995) support empirical links between HRM practices and firm performance. Arthur (1994) collected data from 30 US steel mills, and the research shows that the mills with commitment systems (focus is on developing committed employees who can be trusted to use their discretion to carry out job tasks in ways that are consistent with organisational goals) had higher productivity, lower scrap rates and lower employee turnover than those with control systems (enforcing employee compliance with specified rules and procedures and basing employee rewards on some measurable output criteria). A study conducted by Ichniowski et al. (1995) presents the following conclusion:

> The adoption of a coherent system of these new work practices, including work teams, flexible job assignments, employment security, training in multiple jobs, and extensive reliance on incentive pay, produces substantially higher levels of productivity than do more 'traditional' approaches involving narrow job definitions, strict work rules, and hourly pay with close supervision. (p.1)

Schuler and Macmillan (1984, p.242) argue that 'effective management of human resources gives benefits which include greater profitability'. They have gone on to ponder whether effectively managing human resources has a positive impact on the firm's overall success through improving productivity, achieving and sustaining competitive advantage, and assuring workforce flexibility. Lengnick-Hall and Lengnick-Hall (1998, p.468) suggest that 'organisations which engage in a strategy formulations process that systematically and reciprocally considers human resources and competitive strategy, will perform better over the long term'.

The study conducted by Huselid (1995) provides broad evidence that the use of high-performance work practices results in better firm performance. He found that high-performance work practices include comprehensive employee recruitment and selection procedures, incentive compensation and performance management systems, and extensive employee involvement and training. Ichniowski et al. (1995) conclude that the use of progressive HRM practices is associated with both high productivity and high financial performance in 65 business units.

The above literature provides some evidence that there is a link between SHRM and firm performance. There is a problem of measuring the bottom-line impact of SHRM, as many other variables also affect organisational performance. It is difficult to isolate the impact of one specific strategy from other strategies.

2.6 Management accounting and strategic human resource management

Achieving a competitive advantage through SHRM places an increased emphasis on the need for organisations to take a more strategic approach to managing their employees (Ezzamel et al., 1995). If SHRM is going to be integrated into corporate strategy, MA is one means of reporting the HRM–organisational performance link. As Purcell (1995, p.84) argues, 'the challenge of human resource management is to show a link between policy, practice, and organizational outcomes that is meaningful to the corporate board'. That is a possible role for MA.

Armstrong (1989) notes that the decision about organisational structures and process, and the treatment of employees, are as much influenced by accountancy logic as by HR strategy principles, such that 'the treatment of human resources becomes an instrument for the achievement of accounting targets' (p.164). Armstrong (1995, p.144) argues that 'over the past two decades there has been a spectacular increase in the sophistication and prominence of accounting control in British companies'. He further points out that management accountants play a key role not only in the formulation of overall company strategy, but also in measuring performance and controlling HRM activities. He also suggests (p.150) that the outcome (performance) of HRM activities can be reported in accounting terms.

Armstrong (1995) and Townley (1995) point out the widespread use of accounting information as a key management control device. For example, MA plays a key role in the development of budgetary targets used not only to control department managers, but also to develop measures of departmental performance. Armstrong also suggests that, in order to improve performance, HR managers must be able to understand the language of MA.

More recently, an Australian case study conducted by Howes (1997) identified a range of key factors that impact on HR strategy. The two important factors are, first, external environmental factors and, second, internal HR benchmarking measures. These factors – for example, absentee rates, cost of selection, percentage of internal promotions to external recruits and training and development expenditure – are considered important in determining HR strategy. Thus, in determining these factors and measures, Howes suggests that management accountants must make a contribution. The role of the management accountant is not to take on the role of HRM strategy formulation, but rather to be an active player providing the information required in the planning and controlling of the strategy (Bromwich and Bhimani, 1994).

Another important area for MA concerns the difference between the 'hard' and 'soft' versions of HRM: 'The "hard" variant of HRM might be regarded as the logical end-product of the strategy of justifying personnel management through accounting indices' (Armstrong, 1995, p.150). Management accountants can also provide information on the soft version of HRM: for example, providing information in setting up the budget for a reward system – a soft version of motivation and commitment by employees (Armstrong, 1995). Some Japanese companies have a more direct link between corporate strategies and MA compared with their Western counterparts. Japanese companies may use the accounting system to motivate employees – more of an 'influencing role' than an 'information role' in the managerial process (Hiromoto, 1988).

2.7 Overview

The above literature review suggests that SHRM is being increasingly recognised as one of the most dynamic areas of organisation and plays a key role in meeting the challenges posed by constant external and internal environmental changes in responding to new and qualitatively different competitive conditions. SHRM is identified as one critical component of any organisation's strategy where the expanded role of MA can play a key business partnership role. There is a shortage of empirical evidence that can be used to provide comprehensive descriptions of the practice of MA in relation to SHRM. However, relatively new theoretical models of SHRM and SMA add to our understanding of how organisations manage and monitor their scarce resources to gain and sustain competitive advantage. It can be suggested that MA information is of vital importance to HRM decision-making to ensure the success and survival of organisations in competitive environments.

Introduction to the Case Studies

The literature review, together with analysis of the data and findings of both the UK and Canadian surveys, provided the basic foundations in gaining an understanding of the role of MA in relation to SHRM and constituted the stage for selection of leading-edge companies.

The criteria for selection of the case study sites were as follows:

- two of the top 500 UK companies and two of the top 500 Canadian companies;
- a minimum of 1000 employees for each case.

The companies with a minimum of 1000 employees would provide the HR strategies needed to identify the role of MA in the HR strategic process.

The type of sampling 'is based on the assumption that one wants to discover, understand, gain insight; therefore one needs to select a sample from which one can learn the most' (Merriam, 1988, p.48). The information for research sites selection was obtained from the questionnaire survey respondents who agreed that their company could be considered as one of the research sites. The questionnaire surveys, which preceded the in-depth case studies, constituted a knowledge-gathering tool.

A letter outlining the purpose of the research was sent to an appropriate executive of the organisation. Because of the nature of the study, the criteria for the selection of interviewees were:

- human resource management;
- management accounting;
- users of management accounting information.

The criteria varied slightly according to the organisation: for example, in a logistics business the interviews were conducted at various business units or depots with site managers and line personnel. On average, two weeks were spent on-site collecting data through various methods, such as, personal interviews and site tours (details are provided in the individual case study chapters).

3 Case Study No. 1: Royal Mail

3.1 Research site

3.1.1 Overview

Royal Mail (RM) is one of the largest businesses within the UK Post Office Group, providing a wide range of mail services to its social and business customers. The Post Office Group is a publicly owned corporation and has a total of four businesses (Figure 3.1) each of which has its own managing director, namely:

1. Royal Mail.
2. Parcelforce World-wide.
3. Post Office Counters Ltd.
4. Subscription Services Ltd.

Figure 3.1 The Post Office Group

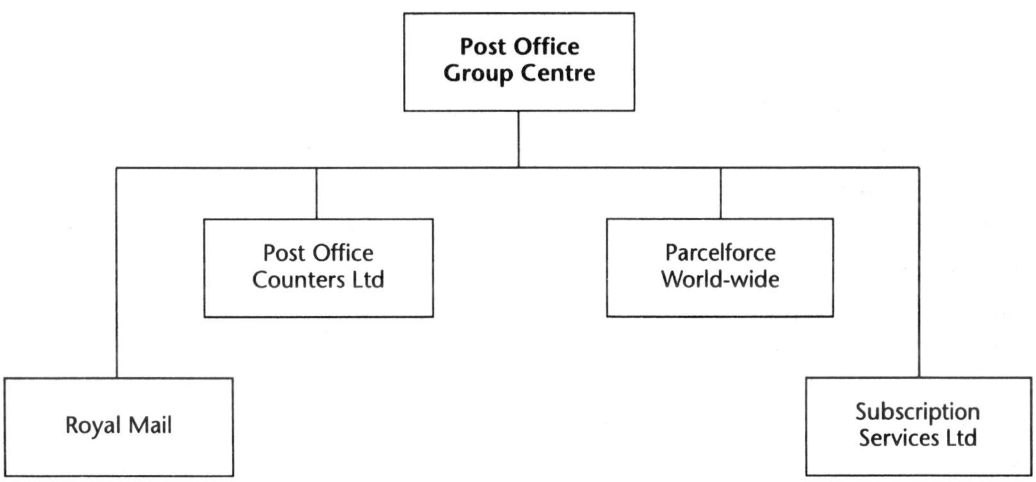

3.1.2 Organisation

The RM is organised into Royal Mail Strategic Headquarters (SHQ) and business units of nine divisions with the same organisation structure for each division (Figure 3.2). Royal Mail Scotland and Northern Ireland (Sc&NI) Division is one of nine operating divisions within the Sales and Operations of Royal Mail. The Sc&NI Division is the research site for this case study, though interviews were also conducted at the SHQ. Under the direction of a managing director at SHQ, at the divisional level (Sc&NI) the management team, known as the Divisional Executive Committee, consists of the Director and General Manager, Director of Communications, Director of Operations

Performance, Director of Operations Programmes, Director of Asset Performance, Director of Finance, Director of Planning and Integration, Director of Sales and Customer Services and Director of Personnel (Figure 3.2). Each of these directors has administrative support staff. Operational area managers report to the Director of Operations Performance. There are a total of nine areas within the Sc&NI Division, and within each area there are unit managers.

Figure 3.2 Royal Mail divisional structure

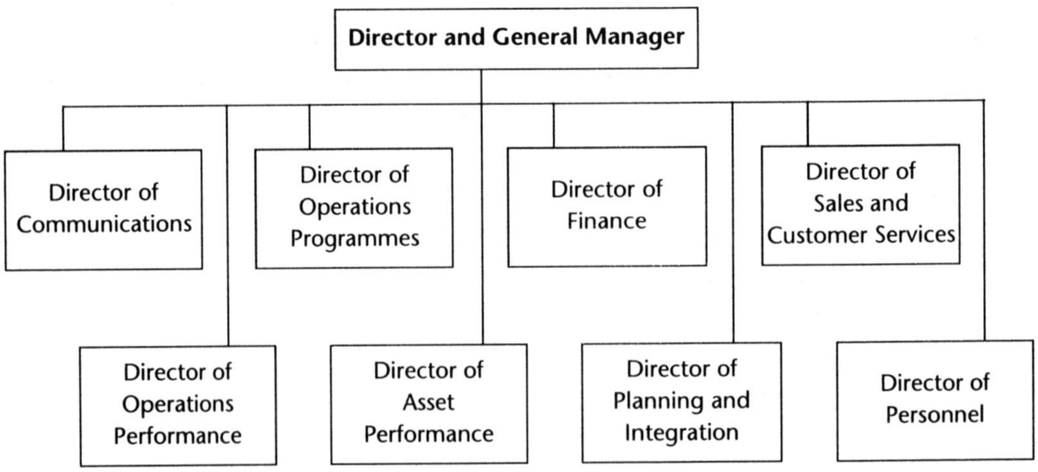

3.1.3 Business details

The RM, with the combination of a focus on core activities and development of new business, continues to deliver profitable growth. The main aim is to grow profitable volume from the organisation's major existing markets and services. Royal Mail emphasises that its success is based on service excellence and customer choice rather than on legal monopoly. Royal Mail is developing innovative solutions to meet customers' evolving needs, to continually improve the service, to promote market growth and to protect its market share. The organisation is increasingly looking to electronic communications to keep in touch with customers and suppliers. The continued growth in the direct mail sector, the UK's third largest advertising medium, is clear evidence of its value as a highly effective channel of communication between businesses and customers. Providing a quality service for RM customers remains a top priority, with a substantial investment in computer and hi-tech interactive technology. A multi-million pound investment both in a new generation of mail processing equipment and in regional sorting centres and delivery offices reflects RM's determination to take advantage of the opportunities offered by technological advances. This, together with the latest tracking and bar-coding equipment, and computerised route planning, boosts quality of service and efficiency, and keeps down costs.

Royal Mail's developing business partnerships with customers such as Help the Aged, BT and the BBC help to stimulate new and improved products, services, ideas and, ultimately, customer satisfaction. The business's priority next-day service in partnership with Post Office Counters has already proved popular with customers, and is growing all the time.

During 1994/95, RM comfortably beat its annual return on capital employed target, achieving 29.2 per cent against its 14.5 per cent target.

The Sc&NI Division has a number of significant features:

- *The geography.* The division covers two countries and 38 per cent of the UK landmass, but only 12 per cent of the population.
- *The customers.* There are 166,000 registered businesses and the divisional sales team manages 1432 of their top customers.
- *The suppliers.* Over £38.1m was spent with over 2760 suppliers in Sc&NI. The top 161 suppliers accounted for 80 per cent of this expenditure
- *The operation.* RM has approximately 166,000 employees, with 16,000 employees at the Sc&NI Division. The division has 203 delivery offices and 5 mail processing centres in Aberdeen, Belfast, Edinburgh, Glasgow and Inverness. Over 1.6 billion letters are posted each year in Sc&NI, with 1.0 billion delivered in Sc&NI.
- *Financial performance.* The Sc&NI Division existed as a distinct business from 1992. From 1992, the division has been a profit centre and is assessed on a contribution and not just a cost basis. The key financial results show that the division has achieved significant improvements in performance over the last five years, with a £3m reduction in the cost of support services. For the first time since 1992, the contribution exceeded targets in both 1996/97 and 1997/98.
- *Competitive strengths.* The Royal Mail's competitive strengths are:
  - scale of operations – its cost structure and high and growing volumes give low and falling unit costs, enabling it to offer competitive prices in all markets;
  - scope of operations – its capabilities of handling a diverse range of different services through the same or broadly similar pipelines;
  - reach of unique national networks – it delivers to every address in the UK;
  - reputation of people – its employees are trusted members of the local community;
  - familiar and trusted brand – its brand image is strong, reflecting the organisation's role in the life of the nation;
  - resources – it has substantial physical and human resources, including unique expertise.

3.2 Primary data

3.2.1 The interviews

The interviews were conducted at the Sc&NI divisional and strategic headquarters offices. Notes were taken during the interviews, and all interviews were recorded. These interviews were later transcribed. The interviews were conducted over a full-time two-week period. The minimum time for each interview was about an hour and some interviews lasted for a morning or afternoon. The profile of the interviewees is as follows (HR = human resource; MA = management accountant; US = user of management accounting information):

1. Manpower Planner (HR).
2. Director of Personnel (HR).
3. Head of Employee Relations (HR).
4. Personnel Assistant (HR).
5. Group Reporting Manager (MA).
6. Director of Finance (MA).
7. Divisional Reporting Manager (MA).
8. Costing Manager (MA).
9. Divisional Development Manager (US).
10. Information Systems Manager (US).
11. Director of Business Planning and Integration (US).
12. Planning Analyst (US).
13. Operations Performance Manager (US).

3.3 Policies and strategies

The guidelines issued by RM's Strategic Headquarters (SHQ) are accessible on the national initiative database, which was set up as an improvement following a review of past planning process cycles. The guidelines are derived from the planning architectures and initiatives and are consistent with the organisational *purpose, direction, values and goals.*

The *purpose* is to develop and provide quality, affordable and trusted service throughout the UK and the rest of the world. The organisational *direction* is to grow profitable volume, and protect and promote market growth from the current markets and services based on service excellence and customer choice in order to meet the growing competition. The organisation is committed to improving the service continuously and developing innovative services to meet customers' evolving needs.

The RM has a set of business *values* (Focus on Customers, Respect and Price) to which all of its employees must adhere. They describe the way in which everyone in RM must behave when dealing with customers, with suppliers and with each other. These key values are essential if RM is to achieve its purpose and direction. In this case it is important to recognise that the business strategies are developed under the policy and procedures from SHQ. These business strategies are directly linked to the organisational strategic goals. At the divisional level (Sc&NI) the company's purpose, direction and values *(PDV)* are set out in nine strategic goals by the divisional directors. At the Divisional Executive Committee Group workshop, the *nine strategic goals* are grouped into *five key divisional strategies*, which are linked to the PDV, set out by SHQ (Figure 3.3). The five key divisional strategies that are linked to corporate PDV are then cascaded into a strategic programme and ultimately into measurement points at the divisional level (Figure 3.4).

Figure 3.3 Five key divisional strategies (nine key strategic goals are grouped into the key divisional strategies)

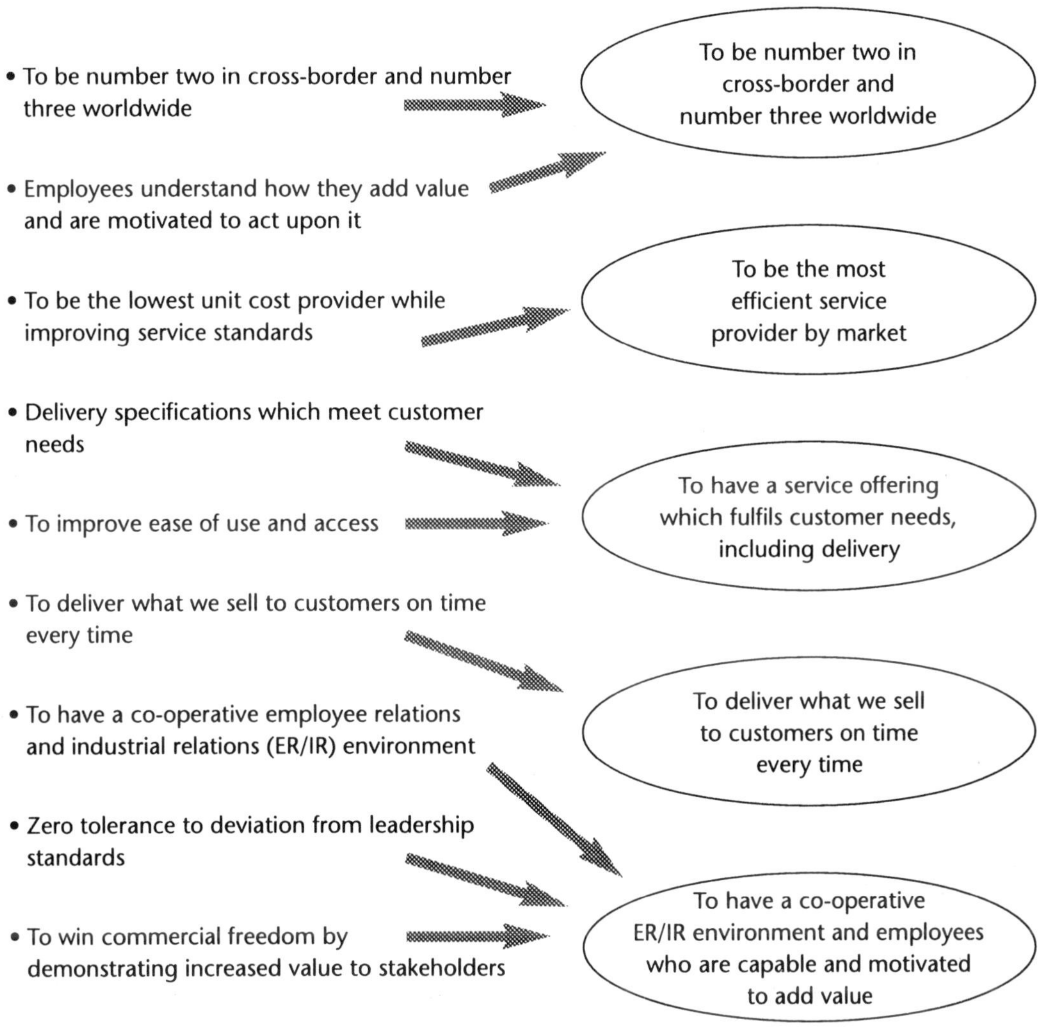

Figure 3.4 Cascade of strategies to strategic programme

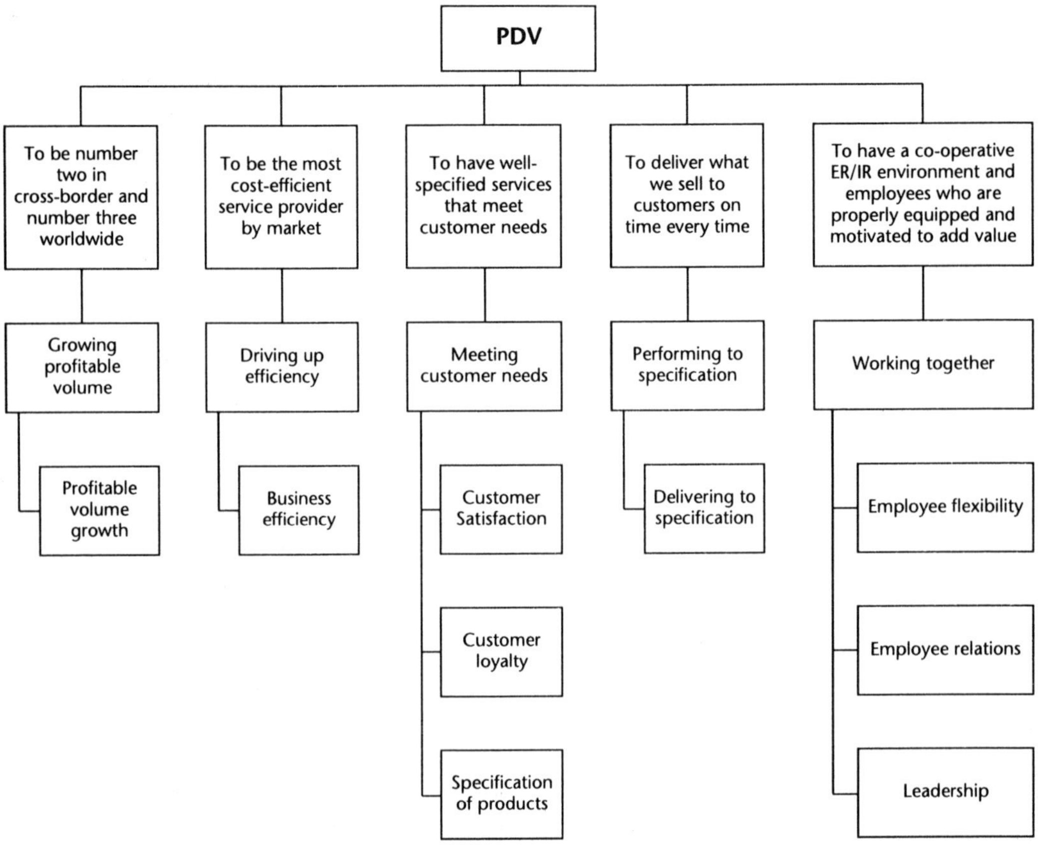

3.4 Results

This section presents the results of the data collected by interviews as well as documents collected from the site. The analysis results are grouped into categories and subcategories from the concepts in accordance with the procedures of coding and the method of analysis used by Strauss and Corbin (1990).

The abbreviations introduced in the respondent profile section are also used here to identify individual comments. Part A (section 3.4.1) represents the *grouping of strategies* identified as *HR strategies* important to respondents, and Part B (section 3.4.2) represents the *grouping of contributions* identified as *MA contributions in relation to HR strategies*. In the final stage of analysis, the strategies are integrated with the MA contributions (see Figure 3.10).

3.4.1 Part A: Human resource strategies

Quality of service

The philosophy behind the strategy of quality is

> that at the end of the day, the focus is to increase market focus and profitability and how they get to that is by customer long-term loyalty and be in line with

> competitive advantage in the marketplace by providing customer service that is right the first time, listening to the customers, get feedback via Customer Perception Satisfaction Index (CPSI), finding out what the customer wants, fulfilling customer needs. (US3)

The strategy for quality is initiated and developed by management at SHQ. US3 explained that this strategy is built into the divisional business planning and is very much in line with the PDV mission of SHQ. US3 responded with respect to quality: 'an instrument designed for customers, what we call, "Customer Perception Satisfaction Index (CPSI)", and have had in place for a number of years'. CPSI is to get feedback from customers over time and US3 identified its importance as, 'that is a big driver for our plan in terms of setting targets and activities'. The 1997 RM survey results showed 1 per cent above the national increase. The division also achieved the second highest improvement in the customers' perceptions of the relationship with the RM.

The quality of service performance is measured by comparing quality of service with real unit cost. The quality of service rises as cost per unit goes down, primarily by getting things right first time and avoiding rework. As a result the cost per item of handling mail has fallen every year. The real unit cost reduction has been a very positive trend since 1989, as has been the rise in quality until 1996/97, and there is a significant rise in service to customers. As can be seen in Figure 3.5, the comments relating to the strategy 'quality' can be analysed into sub-strategies. The results of this strategy through customer satisfaction, which is measured by CPSI, are some of the strategic goals built from PDV.

Figure 3.5 'Quality' strategy

Leadership

The Agenda for Leadership strategy was initiated during 1997 and came about from the RM Executive Committee at the SHQ (US3, MA1, HR1, MA2, HR2 and MA2). Royal Mail Sc&NI issued the 1998 Business Excellence Review document for their leadership strategy: 'Understanding customers, needs and developing their loyalty through the quality of the services we supply rather than relying on our traditional monopoly, is key to our future success.'

According to the key process plan for the division document for 1998/99–2000/01, the leadership strategy is designed for people management, 'to develop leadership qualities in all our managers to ensure that they operate consistently within the Leadership Charter and Business Excellence Review Model, through providing training and development opportunities, encouraging the use of key capabilities and deploying leadership training process'.

The Agenda for Leadership strategy is developed at SHQ and fits in with the vision statement, Purpose, Direction and Values. MA1 explained that the objective of the leadership strategy is to give managers leadership training, and 'to get people in position to qualify for the managerial positions'.

US1 expressed his views: 'Leadership Strategy is nationally driven and the emphasis on leadership strategy is to improve management stock. Ultimate objective is to have better [leading] people and a better stock of managers, taking charge of ultimately delivering quality of service.' All the managers, including the front-line managers, went through workshops called Self-Assessment, assessing themselves in terms of 'leadership capabilities'. Everyone currently an operational manager has been assessed. The results of the leadership capabilities were classified into three categories: (1) fully qualified, (2) part qualified, and (3) not yet qualified.

HR1 believes that this strategy of leadership is a cultural change. As he described: 'With this Leadership Strategy, we are trying to change the culture of the business. The real objective is the culture. We have what we call Leadership Standards. The main Leadership Standards are (1) developing self, (2) developing a team and (3) developing others.'

The Agenda for Leadership strategy is to develop leadership qualities in all managers to ensure that they operate consistently within the Leadership Charter and Business Excellence Review by providing training and development opportunities, encouraging the use of key capabilities and deploying the Divisional Agenda For Leadership and Effective Leadership Feedback strategies.

HR3 expressed his views on the leadership training success: 'We have been pleased with the success of the Achieving Effective Leadership courses which we have run. We have put almost all [92 per cent] of our middle and senior managers through the Programme and have consistently had very good feedback [92 per cent satisfaction to date].'

US1 identified leadership training as, 'there is a need to develop mechanisms to ensure there is a sufficient stock of fully developed and qualified staff to cover all future requirements at managerial level'. Figure 3.6 shows the Agenda for Leadership strategy's process of assessment, training, development and outcomes leading to PDV.

Figure 3.6 Agenda for Leadership strategy

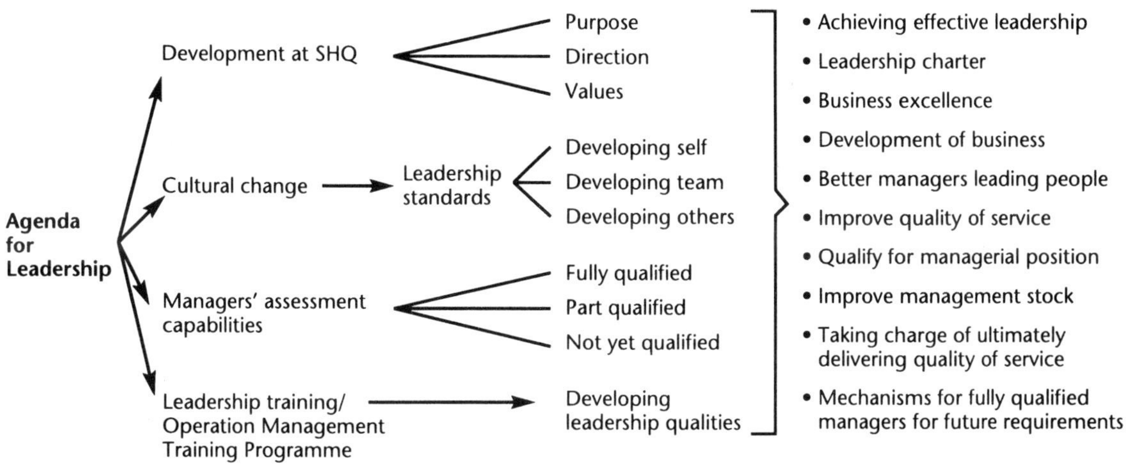

Training and development

The objective of the training and development initiative is to ensure that all staff are equipped with the skills and knowledge required to perform their jobs effectively, in line with RM's Business Mission and Values and with the Business Excellence Review. The Training Partnership has put in place processes and systems to facilitate opportunities for learning and education for all front-line staff. The Royal Mail Executive Committee (RMEC) initiated documents that are developed at the divisional level. Strategy is set out in a framework for the next three years for the development of all staff employed within the division, thereby maintaining a qualified workforce. Within this framework there is full recognition of RM's Purpose, Direction and Values.

After training needs are determined and then translated into objectives, the programmes are developed, planned and executed and finally measured. This evaluation process is an integral part of the training programme. This gives the employees a chance to evaluate and also to choose further improvement programmes. US1 pointed out that 'there is a need to develop mechanisms to ensure there is a sufficient stock of fully developed and qualified staff to cover all failure requirements at managerial levels. Both managers and the front-line people are getting trained, not only leaders, the front-line people are getting skills training.'

According to US1, from 1992 to 1995/96 there was gradual erosion of investment in all levels of training and development. In total, the training and development investment was £3m p.a. or 0.8 per cent of the division's total expenditure. This position was reversed during 1996/97 and into 1998, with training and development now regarded as fundamental. In total, the yearly investment for training and development stands at £7.5m p.a. or 1.8 per cent of divisional expenditure. This represents an increase of £4.5m p.a. over the previous period. By the year 2000 this will have increased again, with the yearly investment standing in the region of £13m p.a. According to US1, training and development is their ongoing strategy and is considered to be a major investment with a very high priority.

US1 further added, 'Our high-performance strategy is: a commitment to training – for both managers and non-managers.' As seen from Figure 3.7, the strategy for training and development shows various subcategories or tactics based on comments from the respondents.

Figure 3.7 Training and development strategy

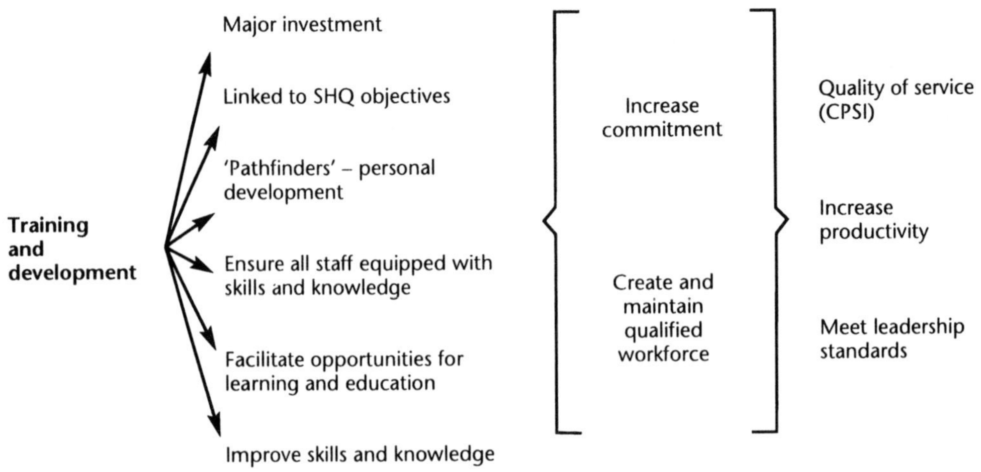

Employee relations

The employee relations (ER) strategy is to optimise the contribution of employees to achieve customer satisfaction using an Employee Opinion Survey and other key measures as a key driver in developing policies and plans. Improving ER has been a high priority in recent years, and a number of initiatives directly aimed at achieving this goal are underpinned by the Sc&NI Division. The ER strategy focuses on increasing employee involvement and employee satisfaction that will increase customer satisfaction. HR3 explained the involvement concept of the ER strategy: 'This is about communication, openness, trust and issues around that sort with employees.' US1 stated:

> for future years the three areas on which we need to focus are recognition, leadership and communications. The focus is how we get our employees much more involved. What we need to do is get the employees involved in what we do in the business. If we can get them involved in every possible way, whether it be sports, social functions, activities or community involvement and building team concept. The result of improved ER should be greater employee commitment with a resultant improvement in business performance, a drive towards achieving competitive advantage.

Figure 3.8 illustrates that the objective of ER strategy is to get employees involved, increase employee commitment, encourage social functions, provide adequate health facilities and practise equal opportunities. These areas are measured by an Employee Opinion Survey. The outcome of the measurement is how employees feel about leadership and communication that lead towards business improvement through employee satisfaction.

Figure 3.8 Employee relations strategy

Flexibility

MA1 believes that there is going to be competition in the near future, and in order to get ready, 'our main resources are people – our main cost driver is people', so what they are aiming for is flexibility, 'partly to satisfy the customer and partly to get our people committed'. MA1 emphasises what flexibility would do for the organisation: 'with this flexibility it will help to achieve what the customer wants and I think flexibility will help'. Further, he states: 'people are our organisation, they are the organisation. If people think we aren't right, then we won't deliver their mail to their satisfaction.'

US3 pointed out that flexibility is one of the three big strategies at the moment. An ER manager expressed his views: 'in order to be competitive, one of the keys is flexibility in the workforce'. HR3 stated: 'the importance of flexibility as one of the keys for our capability to respond quickly'. HR3 emphasised the importance of flexibility to gain competitive advantage:

> To me flexibility is a major thing, we got to move, we are talking about the workforce. I think the key is our people issues and that is the bottom line. Things change quickly and our people are key to competitive advantage. How important are our people to us, well, I think at the end of the day, our key to everything we do in our organisation is people. We got to get that right. My point is, it is worth continuing investing in people, it pays to build our resources in people.

Figure 3.9 shows the result of employee flexibility is towards driving up business efficiency through responding to change, working together, performing to specification and gaining competitive advantage.

Figure 3.9 Strategy for flexibility

3.4.2 Part B: Management accounting contribution

One of the key questions posed to all the respondents was the role of MA in relation to HR strategies. All the respondents (HR1, HR2, HR2 (second interview), HR3, HR4, MA1, MA2, MA3, MA4, US1, US2, US3, US4 and US5) identified different aspects of the contribution by MA in different domains of the HR strategies.

The MA contributions at different levels are grouped together and given labels of:

- business planning;
- measuring performance, reporting and communicating;
- decision-making.

Business planning

Divisional business plans are prepared at the divisional level under the policy, procedures and guidelines issued by the SHQ. The HR strategies mentioned under 'Policies and strategies' (section 3.3 above) are integrated in building divisional business plans. According to MA1, 'the strategies mentioned above are initiated at a high level here at SHQ and developed by focus groups who are representatives from different disciplines like finance and personnel group'. US3 also responded on planning procedure, where the finance group from the divisional level takes part at the development stage. The process of business planning is a team effort from different areas within the division, including a key role played by MA2 who was a member of a focus group at SHQ. HR2 and MA2 both confirmed that 'HRM and finance work closely together now' in putting the business plan package together.

HR1 expressed his views on the role of MA at the development stage. The strategies are developed and initiated at SHQ level with the members of the RMEC. These members are from different disciplines, including finance and HRM. Before any strategies go to the divisional level, 'management accountants or finance people have a contribution at the level of development and are also part of the decision-making process'; further, 'they provide analysis on cost and benefits'.

US3 supports the contribution from MA: 'So at SHQ, we have management people like a finance analyst who needs to understand what stakeholders and the target and the regime are, also need to understand our current performance and our goals. We need to add value and use capital to achieve our goals.' US3 explained that the plans are developed at divisional level, making sure that they are implemented according to a plan submitted to SHQ, and commented further:

> as we are developing our full plan, management accounting can kick in, in terms of costing, contribution on investment, risk, payback. And they will look at a big picture financially as well as various points. So they would say, in total some of you are ambiguous to do this, and here are the constraints we got. We haven't got that money and therefore our plans are financially driven because finance is our resource.

The planning targets are set by SHQ, and the divisional executive committee develops plans based on those targets. The role of finance people is to give a clear picture with internal targets, in terms of financial appraisal, capital scheme, what it is going to cost, benefits and payback, etc., 'so they would also be involved in the analysis and they would offer advice as we develop our plans and strategies'.

HR1 agreed that management accountants get involved in cost–benefit analysis. MA2 pointed out the financial excellence programme where a number of team leaders were appointed nationally (including a director of finance) to look at mainly finance areas: (a) revenue, (b) expenditure, and (c) management reporting.

The teams consisted of divisional representatives and management people from the other businesses of the Post Office Group. The objective is to come up with different strategies for revenue, expenditure and management reporting areas. This is where the MA contribution at the strategic level and the outcomes from the above are integrated into the strategic business planning.

HR2 argued that 'the role of MA is at the different stages of the strategy. At the divisional planning stage, there are lots of costs implications, for example people costs, and HR need to understand the impact of manpower planning on the bottom line.' HR2 expressed his views on the MA role as 'very much teamwork, they are talking costs, I am talking manpower. We are talking integral things. There is no point in my saying I need 200 people, if we can't afford it.'

Once the business plans are prepared at the divisional level under the guidelines from SHQ, they are presented to the RMEC. The committee consists of managing directors of various disciplines, including finance at SHQ. The representatives of divisional executive committee members present their divisional business plan.

HR1 expressed his views on the contribution from MA:

> We work reasonably close to management accountants and we talk when we require help. Before the guidelines are set out, we need to talk about the guidelines, when the information gets back, we would get together and we would discuss that jointly with finance people. Again, when the budgets are set and approved, we would get together. We work close enough to sort out the problems.

MA1 concluded that financial people are involved at all levels:

> at SHQ here, we look at all our key strategies and make sure that the divisional level has reflected all of the strategies in the business plans. We are talking about including Royal Mail generic strategies namely (1) volume growth, (2) improve efficiency, (3) increase customer satisfaction, (4) improve customer perception, and (5) improve employee relations. We have financial expertise at RMEC [Royal Mail Executive Committee] and at each level within the division. We analyse from this level at SHQ with financial expertise and make sure that it is consistent with what they at the divisional level are saying and have built into plans.

The role of the management accountant during the business planning process is very much as an integral team member with a facilitating role.

Measuring performance, reporting and communicating

All the respondents commented on management accountants' involvement and/or their contribution to different areas of performance measurements. MA3 commented, 'One target for management accountants is to meet each manager personally at least once per year to discuss reports.' Informal communication is at least as important for the management accountants as formal communication.

MA1 explained the reporting procedures. On a monthly basis, SHQ is provided with divisional financial reporting. The standard reporting package, Vital Few, shows key performance indicators prepared at the divisional level, compiled by the management accounting group, with information fed from all levels. MA1 commented, 'it is a team effort'. The Vital Few report shows both financial and non-financial indicators. The key indictors are plotted on a graph showing:

Financial

1. Revenue

Non-financial

2. First-class delivered quality of service.
3. Business Customer Perception Satisfaction Index (CPSI).
4. Head count full-time equivalents (FTEs).
5. Safety accidents and contribution.

The above actual performances for 1997/98 are compared with the 1997/98 target and also with the 1996/97 baseline. The Vital Few report is distributed at SHQ and different groups of users who look at it from their perspective (e.g. the personnel planner) would examine it from a manpower perspective. According to MA1 this reporting package is very important and these reports are analysed and briefed to RMEC by finance and/or personnel group. Management accountants play a key role in providing the above critical information in an effective decision-making process. Certain HR strategic decisions are made from the information provided from the Vital

Few reports; for example, the strategy for the development of training and development based on safety accidents among other information. In addition, the information on head count contributes in manpower planning. These reports also contribute in making decisions in the HR strategy development process, where the management accountant is a key member of the HR strategic management team.

One of the key-reporting packages, called Data Pack, is issued on a monthly basis. The contents of Data Pack are manpower planning, employee relations, personnel services, security, safety, resourcing, training and development, and appeals. For example, the report on training and development shows the number of hours spent and budgeted for each division. The outcome of the training is also monitored; leadership training, management development training programme and time management are plotted on a graph showing the pre-course and post-course results.

HR3 calls the report National Reports. It is designed by SHQ but information is fed from the division and 'this information is compiled by the MA group in co-ordination with other departments within the division'. This is an important package of vital information that has an impact on business strategies and corporate strategies, as effective decisions are made based on information contributed by management accounting.

US1 gave his views of MA: 'There is a bottom-line impact on what we are doing with people. The role for management accountants is more co-operative, talking to each other, more of a partnership role.'

Other divisional reporting pointed out by MA1 and US5 is Monthly Mails Operations Keys and Cash Report. MA1 pointed out: 'This is very critical information as our people costs are very high.' The report provides a cash breakdown, showing ordinary pay, overtime, productivity, other pay and allowances and also gross pay. The report also shows key indicators in percentages; for example, sickness absence as a percentage of ordinary hours, overtime as a percentage of gross hours, scheduled attendance as a percentage of gross hours and training as a percentage of gross hours. The actual (1996/97) percentages of overtime, scheduled attendance, sickness absence and training are also compared with the 1997/98 budget. The information is provided from the operational level and compiled by management accountants and the personnel group for further reporting to SHQ. These reports provide critical information on awareness of any problems such as, 'Why so much overtime?'. This information gives business managers opportunities to assess the problems and take effective decisions. Decision-makers must know where action is required, and that is the contribution from management accounting.

The past year has seen some significant changes within the communications functions, including the establishment of a new integrated team, implementation of communication processes and increased focus on measurement, monitoring and display systems. A number of respondents (HR2, HR3, MA2, US1 and US3) commented on the interactive communications. Even though day-to-day information is fed from the functional level to the area managerial level and then to divisional level, this information is compiled and reported by management accountants. HR2 explained, 'these documents come out and are shared with the executive committee, are also shared with area managers and also with my own team'. Further, she continues, 'it is crucial because if you don't know the outcome, how will you know how you are doing against the target or if you have got problems? Once the information is available, we have a directors' [including finance director] meeting where all the directors discuss the outcome, where we are and what necessary steps need to be taken.'

HR3 and US1 are actually doing team briefing on an ongoing basis right down to the unit level. The communication process not only filtered down but also clearly communicated upwards. On a monthly basis, key performance indicators compiled in the standard reporting format Vital Few are reported to SHQ, and this report is critical. MA1 explained, 'These are very important, I can't do anything without these reports.' The Key Process Plan document combined the statement related to interactive communications training with the 'initiative aimed at front-line managers to drive up their ability to ensure briefing is a two-way process which includes local information and takes on board staff views'.

The role of the management accountant is much closer to a consultant than to a controller. For example, even when measuring performance, the informal communication role of the management accountant is at least as important as the formal reporting role. Management accountants are trying to help managers to improve their performance. As US1 stated above, 'the MA role ... is more of a partnership role'. The management accountant is very much part of the management team.

Decision-making

The management accountants' contribution to the decision on 'casual contracts' was explained by HR2. When planning for the long-term, HR2 came up with a strategy of reducing the number of casual employees and increasing the number of full-time employees to get them committed to the job and to improve the quality of service to customers. This is where management accountants played a key role in contributing information for management to make such a decision.

Another HR strategy, brought up by MA2, is about the reduction of temporary contracts. HR2 explained, 'we realised that having temporary contracts actually cost more. These temporary contract employees were not committed, tended to be not of the best quality and also impacted very heavily on their services.' The main concern was about the quality of service for customers. The strategy was initiated by the Director of Personnel at the divisional level in consultation with the finance department people. Even though it was going to cost more, it would be more beneficial in the long term regarding quality of service and commitment of the workforce, with these employees also being tied into a pension fund. This is an example where the Sc&NI Division developed its own strategy with the assistance of management accountants.

Management accountancy also plays a major part in other projects. HR2 stated, 'this is where we very much work with finance people to look at the people cost of making those major changes because that plays a major part in our decision process'; and the role does not end there, because 'management accountants on an ongoing basis provide information during the project'. Decision-making is another example where management accountants are part of the team and act in an advisory role to managers.

3.5 Summary

The corporate/business strategies are clearly developed by a top management team with members from HRM and MA at SHQ. The HR strategies are fully integrated with the overall SHQ strategies and are mission-driven towards their purpose, direction and values. The RM has adopted a strategic HR approach where HR strategies are linked to corporate goals. The management teams both at SHQ and at the divisional level showed a high commitment in pursuing strategies laid out by SHQ. The deployment of HR strategies was well received and developed in the business plan. The HR strategies were implemented and the performance measures were well communicated at all levels, including SHQ and front-line employees. MA1 commented that to deploy the HR strategies effectively and efficiently there is interdisciplinary interaction between SHQ and the executive group at the divisional level and also between HR and MA staff.

Figure 3.10 shows the integration of the strategies within the Sc&NI Division (section 3.4.1 above). The strategies include employee flexibility, employee relations and leadership, together with training and development, and these strategies contribute towards performing to specification (meeting customer needs), driving up efficiency (i.e. business efficiency) and ultimately growing profitable volume. At the same time there is a contribution towards profitable volume with the establishment of providing quality of service, customer satisfaction and customer loyalty in order to meet customer needs. The integration of the above strategies contributes towards the RM's strategic goals: (1) growing profitable volume, (2) achieving business efficiency, and (3) creating an environment to add value to gain competitive advantage. These goals are then linked to overall corporate PDV. The same model is further developed, integrating management accountants' contribution (section 3.4.2, above) in relation to the HR strategies, using Strauss and Corbin's (1990) Model.

Management accountants contribute at different levels in relation to strategies: for example, at SHQ, Finance (a member of RMEC) contributes to developing strategies that cascade down to divisional level. Also at the SHQ level, management accountants play a role in analysing strategies for decision-making at a high level. Further management accountants from the divisional level take part as members of focus groups to come up with ways and ideas to achieve strategic goals. Here the contribution is made collectively with other members of the focus group to help build and develop strategies. At the divisional level the management accountant, as a key member of the Divisional Executive Committee, plays a key role in all aspects of HR strategies, starting from the planning stage to reporting and communicating at SHQ level.

Figure 3.10 Integration of strategies and management accounting contribution

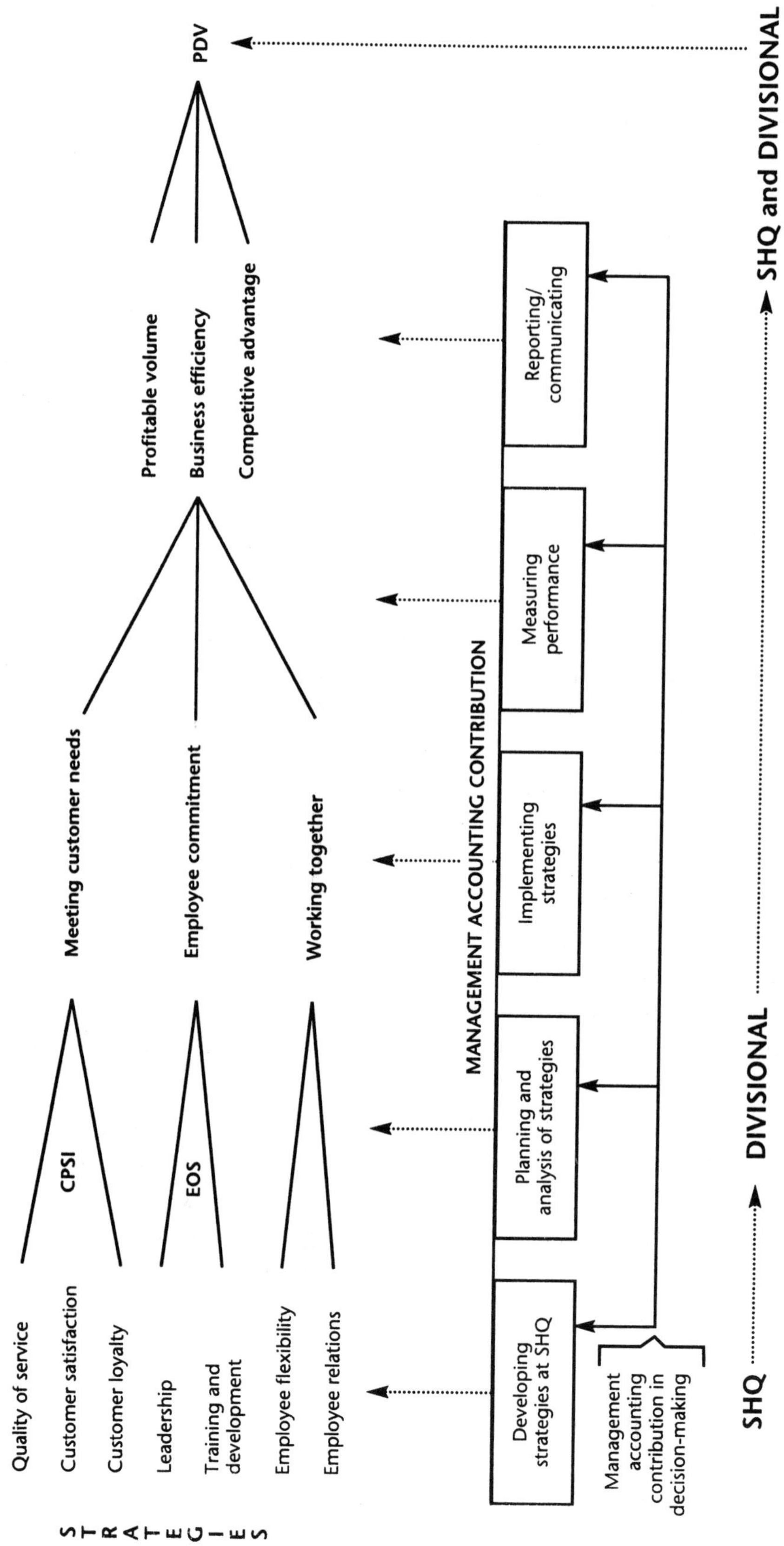

HR1 sees the role of MA as an integrative one:

> we work reasonably closely with management accountants and we talk when we require help. We consult before the guidelines are set out and once the information gets back from SHQ, we would get together and we would discuss jointly with finance people. Also when budgets are set and approved, we would get together and discuss.

The overall views on the role of MA are for management accountants to understand the business, the business strategies, the strategic goals and working with others to achieve those goals. Further, for the *future* role of MA from the managers' perspective, the following are some of the quotes expressed by the respondents:

HR2 is currently happy with the contribution from MA but:

> Our system needs to be faster and more accurate and more easily accessible. I suspect the role of MA should be involved in 'What if' analysis in the future. We are not doing a lot of 'What if' analysis, and that's not just MA, that's all of us.

Her further comment on the future role of the MA:

> the role should be different – a more integrated role and a better information provider.

US2 gave his view on the future role of MA:

> I see the future being, once the system is set up they will get information themselves and the MA role as a consulting role going out and helping out people who manage the budget on a day-to-day business.

HR2 commented on MA role:

> We do have a link with SHQ now, and MA role is business planning process. It is an integrated role, we used to have barriers before, we used to talk about we should do this and that, and the person preparing the plan had no clue. Now we talk openly, and there is no barrier, we have built good relationships with finance people, in the planning process, we set the figures and MA cannot set the figures until we clear them at our end. We need to get compromise and it seems to be working out fine.

MA1, working at SHQ, explained a more collaborative role of MA in future:

> I think it would be useful if we are involved at the earliest stage of the strategic development. So I am not saying one person can do that but I am saying with integration between strategic people at SHQ and MA people. There is MA at strategic level, but an invisible barrier between strategic people and the planning/reporting people. Until those barriers are broken down, you always have a slight disconnection between what they [SHQ] regard as strategies and what operation sides regard as appropriate, operational and achievable strategies. So what I am saying is there should be an integrated role right from the beginning or outset. At the moment, we are sort of running on parallel lines – strategies and operation reporting; and then at some stage we cross, but only at a point in time, but only if we are on the same track, from the outset there would be better understanding and less confusion in our guidelines.

4 Case Study No. 2: Canada Post Corporation

4.1 Research site

4.1.1 Overview

Canada Post Corporation (CPC) is a Crown Corporation established by the Canada Post Corporation Act 1981 to operate a postal service on a self-sustaining financial basis while providing a standard of service to meet the needs of the people of Canada. The subsidiary, PCL Courier Holdings Inc., known as Purolator, is managed independently, also on a self-sustaining financial basis. Together with its affiliated companies, Canada Post ranks thirty-second among Canadian businesses in terms of revenue and is the fourth largest employer in Canada.

4.1.2 Organisation

The Board of Directors of CPC has eleven members, including the President and Chief Executive Officer (CEO). The Chairman of the Board and the President and CEO are Governor in Council appointees. Under the direction of the President and CEO are seven key functional areas. Mail operation, marketing and sales and retail business are also grouped into geographical divisions (Figure 4.1).

4.1.3 Business details

Canada Post Corporation provides products and services in four major service markets: communications, publications, advertising, and physical distribution. Communications includes letter mail, hybrid products and electronic service. Publications consists of domestic and international newspapers. Advertising consists of admail. Physical distribution consists of courier, expedited delivery and parcels. Revenues are also generated from other sources such as mail redirection, money order and postal box rental services, and payments by foreign postal administrations for delivery of their mail in Canada. The Corporation offers customers a network of approximately 20,000 retail points of access. To co-ordinate its operations and provide the control needed to meet its service standards CPC established a National Control Centre in Ottawa. The control centre, in conjunction with regional control centres, monitors the movement of mail 24 hours a day, seven days a week, and allows CPC to counteract difficulties in order to meet its delivery standards. The Corporation has commercial, operational and financial links with over 200 postal administrations around the world.

Figure 4.1 Organisational structure of Canada Post Corporation

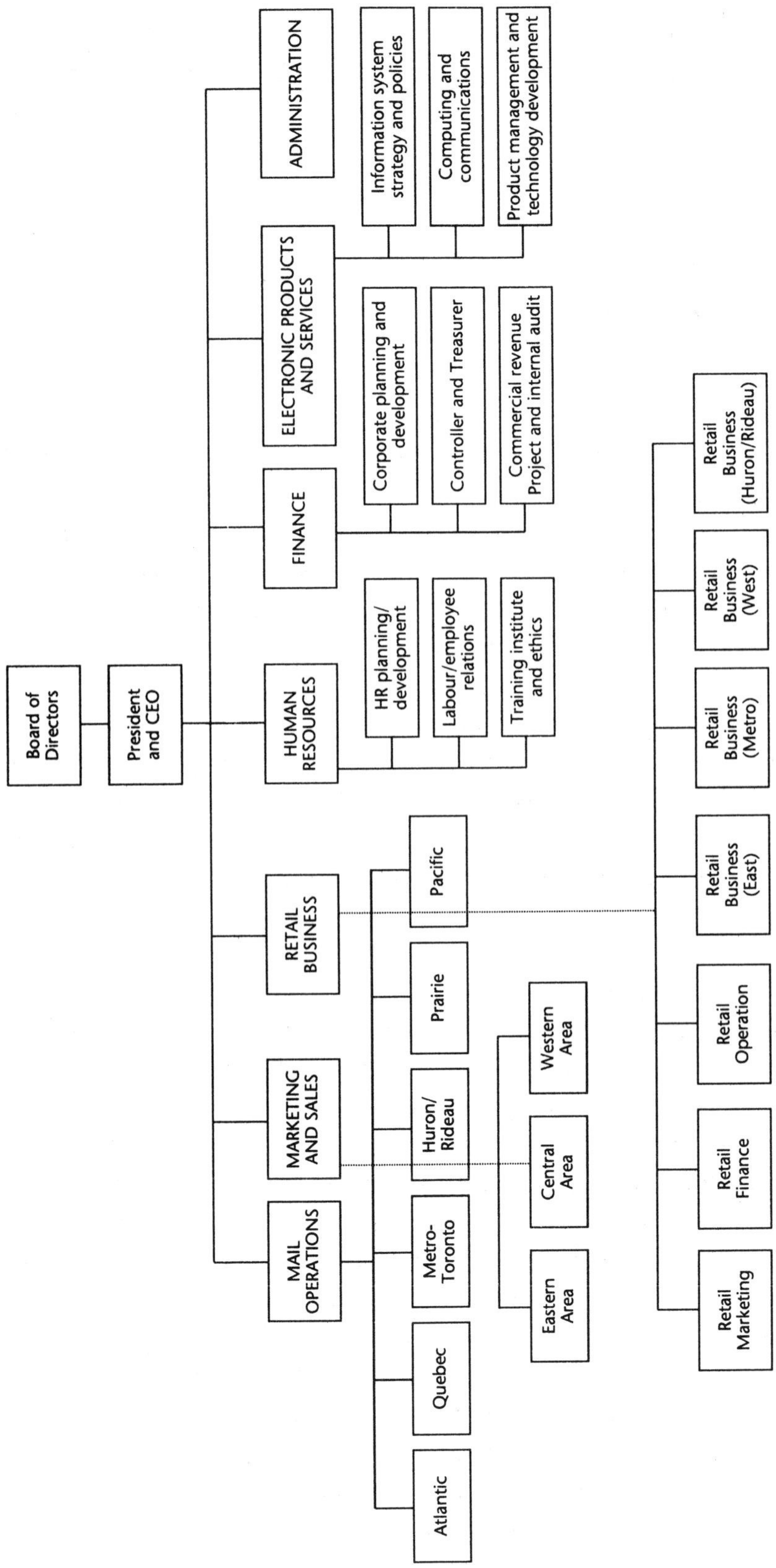

- *The geography.* CPC collects, processes and delivers mail across the world's second largest country (second in geographical size only to Russia).
- *The operation.* CPC delivers an average of 37 million pieces of mail per day, processed through 22 major plants and many other facilities, to over 12.7 million addresses in Canada, and forwards mail to virtually every country in the world. There are over 750 planned domestic flights carrying mail every business day. CPC's fleet of vehicles is among the largest in Canada with over 6000 vehicles, logging more than 76 million kilometres during the year.
- *Financial overview.* CPC collected, processed and delivered 9.23 billion pieces of mail and parcels during the 1997/98 fiscal year. In doing so, they served 30 million Canadians and over 900,000 businesses and public institutions.

  In 1997/98, CPC reported a consolidated net income of $36m on revenues of $5.07b. This represents a decrease of $76m from the previous year's net income of $112m. The company's profit was severely eroded by the two-week strike during the last week of November and early December 1997 and fell well short of its goals. Since its first year of profitability in 1989, CPC has paid $86m in dividends to the people of Canada through the federal government, including a $10m dividend in March 1998.
- *The market segment.* CPC's largest market segment, providing 57 per cent of revenue, is communication services. The segment consists of letter mail, publications mail, electronic and hybrid products. The other 43 per cent of revenue comes from publications, advertising and physical distribution.
- *Employees.* CPC relies upon 63,000 full-time and part-time employees to provide effective communication and delivery services to Canadians. The major operation cost of CPC is salaries and benefits (1997/98, 62.9 per cent). The Corporation estimates that thousands of additional jobs, many of them skilled, are directly and indirectly created by its activities.
- *CPC Learning Institute.* During 1996/97, CPC invested $46m in training for its employees. The Learning Institute (CPC in-house training centre) delivered 16 core programmes to more than 150 groups involving more than half of CPC's management personnel. A wide number of job-specific courses were also delivered to more than 40,000 employees.
- *Employee relations and awards.* CPC annually awards 31 scholarships to student children of employees, as an investment in the benefits of higher education.
  - *The Aboriginal Academic Achievement Award* for the Aboriginal children of employees has been launched, with the first awards to be announced in September 1998. The award is intended to help students with the expenses incurred for higher education.
  - *The Heritage Club* consists of retired corporate employees. In 1998 they logged 26,600 hours advancing the cause of literacy and completed a total of 134,000 hours of volunteer work.

4.2 Primary data

4.2.1 The interviews

The interviews were conducted at CPC's largest mail operation site called Pacific Region, located in Vancouver, British Columbia, and also at CPC's headquarters in Ottawa. The five interviews conducted in Ottawa were with the senior corporate managers (MA3, MA4, US2, HR3 and H4). In total, ten interviews were conducted over a three-week period, with an average duration of just over one hour. The profile of the respondents is as follows:

1. Director Finance, Western Area (MA).
2. Director Finance, Mail Operations (MA).
3. Officer Human Resources (HR).
4. Manager Finance, Retail/Sales (US).
5. Manager, Employee Relations Pacific (HR).
6. Corporate Manager, Retail Finance (MA).
7. Corporate Manager, Mail Operations Finance (MA).
8. Corporate Manager, Corporate Planning (US).
9. Corporate Manager, Employee Relations (HR).
10. Corporate Manager, HR Finance (HR).

4.2.2 Secondary data

Other secondary data such as the organisational chart, annual report and financial performance reports, CPC's mission statement, operating principles and priorities were also obtained from various respondents.

4.3 Policies and strategies

For the most part policies are determined at the headquarters in Ottawa, but CPC has taken an integrative approach to the strategic process, initiated at both corporate and operational levels. The Corporation has also developed five corporate priorities as part of the business direction to develop corporate values. The first priority is called Our People. The president admits that CPC has invested huge amounts in technology and state-of-the-art equipment, but what makes the Corporation one of the best in the country is its people. The second priority is called Our Customer. MA4 simplified the priority with the CPC's mission by saying, 'we have a mission, we have an objective, our mission is to serve people and our objective is to improve customer satisfaction'.

The third priority is long-term financial viability, to achieve returns to meet borrowing requirements, and to convince customers that the training provided and the authority and accountability given to everyone within the corporation will provide the service the customers want. The fourth priority is to push for more decentralisation, in order to ensure that decisions are taken at the lowest possible level, where the effects are felt immediately.

Finally, the fifth priority is to accelerate the development of services for long-term survival. HR3 stated, 'our new partners have tremendous resources, human and financial, and a culture of innovation and risk-taking that we lack. To succeed, we will need to form alliances like those we have sealed in the last few years.'

The mission statement issued in CPC's annual report states:

> We are in business to serve all Canadians, businesses and organizations, through the secure delivery of messages, information and packages to any address in Canada or the world, at a level of quality and value that makes customers want to repeat the experience.

The Corporation faces a competitive world and, in order to survive, the President and CEO expressed his views on how competitors manage: 'Corporations that thrive do so because managers and employees work together toward the same goals. Those same corporations tend also to be the ones that are able to create new jobs and provide employees with pay and benefits that reward their efforts.'

One of the biggest challenges facing CPC today is change. Success depends on CPC's ability to adapt to rapid change in a fiercely competitive world. For CPC the monopoly of the letter is being eroded by new means of communication and the Corporation needs to analyse its competition, define its objectives and provide the means of meeting them. To do so, the Chairman of the Board of Directors expressed his views:

> We need a vision, a dynamic action plan to improve our labour relations, make the most of new technology, diversify our product range and forge strategic alliances. Working as a team – employees, managers and union leaders – will get us there.

4.4 Results

The data analysis approach used here is based upon the work of Strauss and Corbin (1990). Following the format of Case Study No.1 (Chapter 3), this section presents the primary data by grouping the key concepts of apparent importance to respondents into strategies.

Part A (section 4.4.1) represents the strategies and Part B (section 4.4.2) describes the contribution from MA in relation to the HR strategic process. The final section is a summary, together with managers' views on the future role of MA. Respondent references used in this section were introduced with their profile in the above section on the interviews.

4.4.1 Part A: Human resource strategies

Mail Operations Supervisory Development Program

The Mail Operations Supervisory Development Program (MOSDP) is a training programme for employees to develop on-the-job management skills. MA2 explained the importance of supervisory skills at the operation level:

> what we are really trying to stress is that the program is geared towards the people skills, soft skills, communications skills, writing skills, negotiation skills, dealing with management conflict, and in addition, we have also added one more module and that is managing diversity, because of diversity in our workforce.

The programme is the most intensive ever put together by CPC. What makes this programme so unique is the opportunity to combine classroom instruction with hands-on experience. The main thrust of the programme is to encourage supervisors to manage their people with superior management skills. While they are away on training, supervisors previously trained in MOSDP fill in at their jobs, and when the supervisors in MOSDP return to their job to do work assignments for their training, they do so in the company of a fully trained coach.

MA2 added the concept of 'lean thinking' at the operation level that is built into the MOSDP for every employee. Lean thinking is 'changing peoples' thinking, ways of creating efficiency'. The same issue of lean thinking was also brought up by MA5, about the way of thinking and looking at what one does at work and how to create value-added activities.

The new graduates from MOSDP found that the programme is designed to help them improve work processes and interpersonal relations in their areas by becoming better managers. The feedback given by the graduates shows the positive effectiveness of this unique programme.

More than 1500 supervisors will go through MOSDP in the next three years, learning leadership, business and communications skills. MA2 identified the total costs for supervisory training just for the Pacific Region: 'My budget is about 1.5 million dollars a year, just for that program, that is not counting all of the other training that is going on in the corporation.' Figure 4.2 opposite summarises the strategy of MOSDP to provide training in order to become a better supervisor with superior management skills.

Human Resource Planning and Development Program

The main objective of the Human Resource Planning and Development Program (HRPDP) strategy is to translate corporate priorities and business plans into work activities, and training and development plans. It is a partnership between the employee and the team leader (anyone with people management responsibilities). HR3 explained the process of HRPDP strategy with five key steps:

1. Setting objectives, performance measurements and action plans.
2. Reviewing competencies needed for the current position.
3. Preparing employee training and development plan.
4. Giving and receiving performance feedback, review and evaluation.
5. Using the career network – ongoing self-directed career management.

Figure 4.2 The Mail Operations Supervisory Development Program

Competencies are the knowledge, skills, abilities and personality attributes associated with a position. According to MA2, rapidly changing technology requires that employees possess the knowledge, skills and abilities needed to cope with new process techniques. The competency review is a process through which employees with their team leader review the competencies needed for their job or position. It is then used to support the continued training and development of employees. It is also important, according to HR3, for team leaders to have a clear idea about the competencies required for employees to carry out their job, their objectives and what training and development plans might be considered. The team leaders then integrate the group's training and development plan with business plans to ensure consistency with corporate goals and directions.

MA3 stressed the ultimate objective of this HR strategy: 'HRPDP strategy is for personal development, you set your objectives, get the necessary training and it's a motivation thing for them, the ultimate objective is for them to be more committed to their job.' MA1, who is responsible for a commercial operation for Western Canada, added that HRPDP strategy is used to help sales people expand their markets. HR2 raised the issue of key indicators that would give good feedback on the impact of key strategies focused on employees. The completed questionnaires are compiled and the results (Employee Satisfaction Index, ESI) are distributed to appropriate personnel for improvements. He also commented that 'our biggest cost is people. And I think the ESI indicator is a key measure of employee satisfaction.'

The Corporation would like to achieve employee satisfaction levels in the 70 per cent, even 80 per cent level. HR3 said, 'we have a target of perfection, of course, our current level is about 55 per cent satisfaction which is not enough, we want to be in the 80s'. According to CPC's Performance Special Report, there is a relationship between employee satisfaction and profitability: the more satisfied employees are, the better the service to customers, and thus the higher the return in customer loyalty. The results of the ESI are based on CPC's focus on employees, improvement, customers and how employees feel about their job. The establishment of the ESI in 1995/96 recognised and built on the important relationship between customer satisfaction and employee satisfaction.

The overview of the process of HRPDP strategy and its outcome is illustrated in Figure 4.3.

Figure 4.3 Human Resource Planning and Development Programme (HRPD)

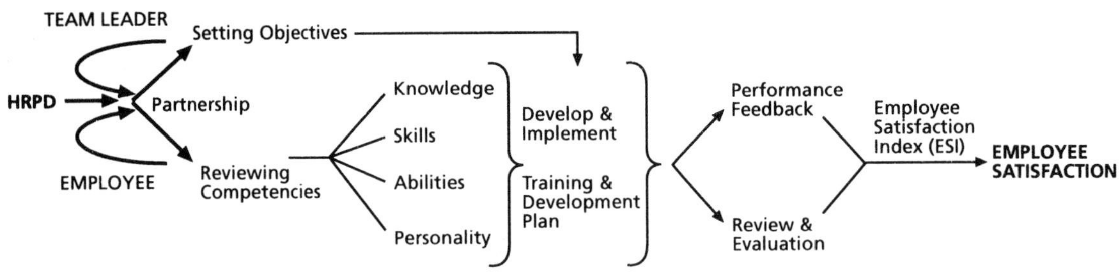

CPC Leadership Profile – Training and Development

For its training and development strategy, CPC has developed a document called CPC Leadership Profile – Training and Development. Specifically, HR3 went into the detail of explaining how the CPC Leadership Profile concept works. This profile has been established as an attainable ideal in management behaviour in all functions of CPC. The behaviour indicators for leadership are driving forward customer value, to act with confidence in challenging the status quo and in setting the example of competence, commitment, customer focus and accountability for results. Finally, the concept for people management is towards respect for individual needs, aspirations and expectations, while ensuring commitment to and delivery on a customer-focused vision. HR3 explained:

> the Leadership Profile is essentially a document which describes the types of behaviour we expect from anyone who is in a people management situation. It is a fundamental instrument as a basis for training, succession planning and developing high potential individuals against that profile.

According to HR3, the CPC Leadership Profile document shows three key areas: (1) leadership, (2) teamwork, and (3) people management. These three key areas are built upon CPC operating principles and corporate priorities. HR4 provided information on how the CPC Leadership Profile is used for training and development: 'we are trying to train all the employees from top down, all the way through to be more in line with Leadership Profile and to be basically more customer-oriented and service-oriented'. According to HR4, the emphasis of the strategy is placed on people focus and improving skills.

The Corporation's Learning Institute (in-house training) is dedicated to aligning CPC's business priorities and training programmes in business management, people management, communication, continuous improvement and team-building. In 1997/98, the institute delivered 16 programmes to more than 150 groups, comprising half of CPC's management. In addition, functional training was delivered to more than 40,000 employees. In CPC's Annual Report the importance of employees is stressed: 'The creativity and knowledge of our workforce is the foundation that strengthens our links with our customers.'

The 1997/98 Customer Satisfaction Index (CSI) is produced quarterly by an independent firm based on random interviews with some 1350 large and small businesses and consumers. Information is gathered by asking customers to assess CPC according to their own priorities and criteria. The Corporation closed the year with a CSI of 65 per cent against a target of 62 per cent. The CSI level showed customer satisfaction rising well beyond the target, reflecting CPC's efforts in keeping its customers informed. In order to continue working hard, the target for 1998/99 is set at 72 per cent.

Figure 4.4 shows the CPC Leadership Profile – Training and Development strategy, as explained by HR3.

Figure 4.4 CPC Leadership Profile – Training and Development

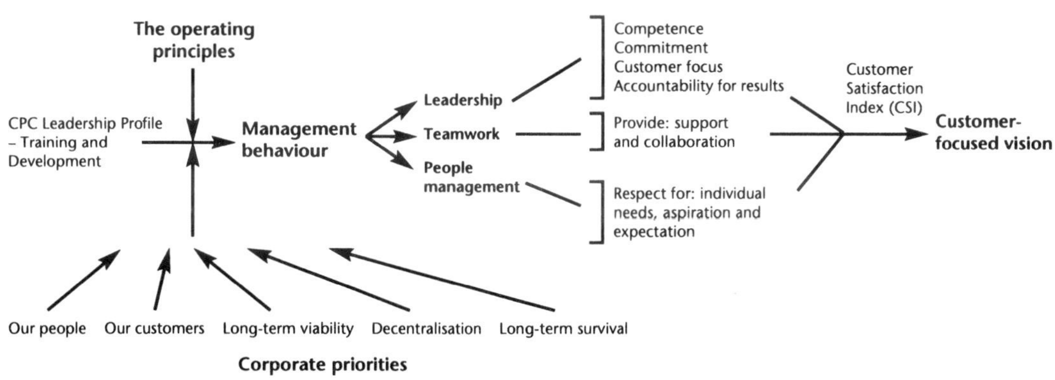

Employee Recognition Program

According to HR3 the Employee Recognition Program (Figure 4.5, overleaf) has been developed to recognise teamwork and individual effort, 'employee recognition which is very important for us and we have quite an elaborate employee recognition program'. HR3 elaborated on the importance of the recognition program: 'every day, countless co-workers go the extra mile, and these day-to-day efforts also deserve to be recognised'. The recognition programme of Postmark Award – a Bravo! praise from a team leader – heightens the sense of satisfaction for a job well done. It is a way of saying 'thank you'. Through the Heritage Club, CPC recognises significant milestones in service to the Corporation – 25, 30, 35, 40 and 45 years. Team leaders are encouraged to be aware of employees reaching these milestones and to add their personal congratulations. To recognise employee excellence, during 1997/98, 195 employees received Golden and Silver Postmark Awards for such achievements as outstanding customer service, commitment to service standards, business growth and leadership. The Postmark Awards are employee-driven, and every employee has an opportunity to recognise colleagues' contribution. The Postmark Awards are divided into categories that include leadership, outstanding customer service, commitment to service standards, business growth, sales award of the year, personal merit, volunteer services, Heritage Club involvement and partnership in service.

MA2 also brought up the issue of the recognition programme at the operation level for their sales representatives, 'our vice-president of sales has implemented a recognition program, for our sales people who are not on commission bases, but they are straight salary and fairly good salary plus good benefits and a car allowance'. So to motivate these sales people, the management has set the sales targets. She explained how this works:

> the positive incentives are, what the management has implemented in the recognition program, a part of the recognition program called the 100 per cent Club, what that means is that anybody who meets 100 per cent of their plan [target] is included in the 100 per cent Club. For those who reach above their target, get special recognition, called Club Excellence.

Figure 4.5 Employee Recognition Program

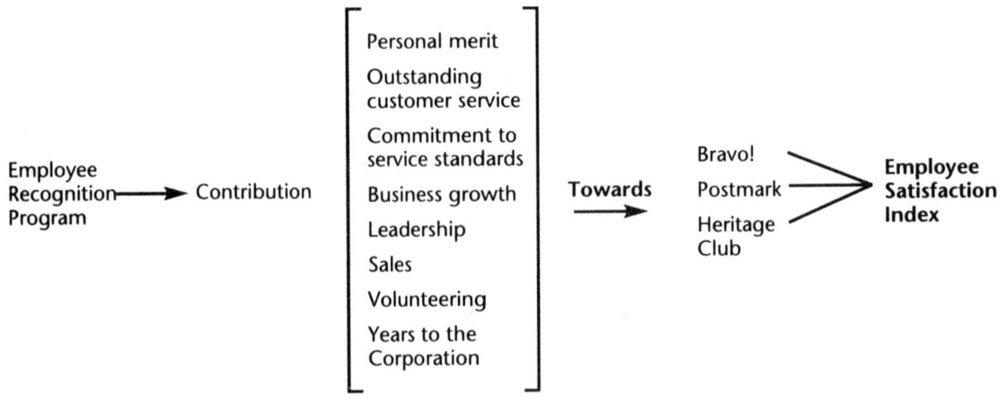

4.4.2 Part B: Management accounting contribution

Part B represents the MA contribution in relation to the key HR strategies identified by respondents. The MA contributions at different levels are then grouped together and given labels as follows.

Business/strategic planning

The CPC has taken an integrated approach that combines both the top-down and bottom-up planning process. The concept of the HR strategies is initiated by the management at both the operational and the corporate levels. At the corporate level they have a committee, known as the Management Executive Committee (MEC), with members from all disciplines. The HR strategies are then built into the operational business plan approved by the MEC at the headquarters in Ottawa. With the above planning approach, there are two different levels of the planning process: (1) strategic level, and (2) operational level.

At the strategic level, US2 (Senior Corporate Manager, Corporate and Strategic Planning) identified that strategic planning is one of their most important responsibilities. US2, with a team of six directors, provides a strategic foundation for co-ordinating and directing the activities of the corporation to achieve the strategic goals.

US2 explained that special attention is given to understanding the planning process at both the strategic and the operation levels and they must develop a well-integrated master plan: 'I do have people in my group who also have a very strong operational background.' US2 further explained the strategic planning process and contribution from MA's perspective: 'one of the key areas we are concentrating on is strategic planning' and 'strategic planning is a corporate function, it's not a finance function'. The management accountant is a member of the most senior management group of the corporation, a key player in the strategic planning process, providing a lot of research, competitive and marketing analysis and contributing to strategic decision-making. US2 explained her contribution by saying:

> to support the senior executives in making decisions on their strategic future. We, as a Corporate Strategic planning group, put a lot of strategic thinking into driving the strategic plan forward. Further, we certainly know what level of service we want to provide to customers and we measure that very closely, we have a vision that we want to be successful.

Finally, US2 expressed her views, 'my role is a very active participation and I believe the role of the finance person is a business manager not as a finance manager, it is critical to understand business in order to provide the information to various people'. US2 concluded that all the strategies, including the HR strategies, developed either bottom-up or top-down, are integrated with the corporate strategic plan. It is important for management accountants to understand what these HR strategies are, the analysis of these strategies and the objectives that are focused towards the overall corporation goals.

At the operational level there is extensive involvement by management accountants. MA3, Manager Finance, Retail/Sales, reporting to Director of Finance, Pacific Region, explained spending 80 per cent of her time supporting commercial operations: 'I do all of the planning, all of the reporting, I think it evolved from spitting out reports to being a partner in decision-making and giving management advice. A lot of the reporting has become automated so what we do is analyse things and work together with managers to increase business.' Further, she stated that:

> our General Manager really believes that our finance group is a part of his management team, although my group don't report to him, he very rarely has a management meeting without me, he really involves us a lot because he feels that we are a big part of his success as well. [And at the same time,] I really feel like I can help him in making decisions and increase his business.

MA2 described her role in the planning process: 'we have taken a bottom-up approach here at the operational level, we start off by looking strategically at the products and where we see there would be growth in British Columbia, with our General Manager and his directors. From there we build our business plan and it goes to the Head Office where the targets are approved by MEC and we make changes as necessary.'

Further, MA2, Director of Finance, Mail Operation, confirmed his role as a key team player: 'My contribution in the planning process, which is very much a bottom-up approach, is largely making sure that number one, it gets pulled together, that it is consistent, fits in with corporate priorities and in the end I am not the only one doing this, we are very much part of the team.'

According to HR4, an important MA contribution is during the planning phase when they are involved in preparing the budget cycle, investment and expected returns. HR4 elaborated further: 'all the projects and investment plans need to be supported by a business case and there is a distinct process where finance groups in each of the functions are responsible for working with their internal client to support and provide a financial analysis point of view in making sure that it integrates'. In addition, at the planning stage, the Director of Finance for the Western Area (MA1) has an intermediary role:

> my role is ever evolving but I sit on a management committee in Western Canada where we determine what the issues of the day are and how we resolve them. We have certain corporate strategies that we want to move forward, we have certain local strategies that we want to move forward, this is the team that makes it happen and I am part of that team. So from that aspect, in a lot of cases we're implementers, lot of cases we are influencers, and in some cases we are designers.

Decision-making

During the course of discussion about the role of MA, MA3 underlined the importance of her role and contribution in decision-making: 'My role being a partner in decision-making and giving advice. We analyse and work together to increase business and I do believe that I can contribute in doing things to increase business, I really believe that the finance group is a part of the management team.' At the regional level the plans are co-ordinated by MA3 with a contribution on setting targets and providing analytical work in decision-making. MA3 gave an example of her contribution in providing general managers with analytical information on setting targets for sales people with respect to the HRPDP strategy and providing her thoughts and views during the decision-making process at the strategic planning stage. The main contribution from MA2 has been from planning, analysing and providing information to making decisions:

> I really think my role is moving away from transactional accounting and moving towards decision-making and that's the key thing. Where I have increased is on my decision-making side. As a finance manager, my main focus is that I am part of a management team that provides advice in order for them to make management decisions.

MA4 strongly believes that, as part of the management team, he plays a major role in every aspect of the decision-making process. He commented, 'my contribution would look at the value of a competition initiative, in planning and implementing and project initiatives, so every step of the way, I think that finance by itself does not exist, finance is basically a reflection of the quality of the line of business projects, and a finance contribution becomes part of the decision'.

Another aspect of the MA contribution is providing information on the Corporation's renewal programme, called Workforce Management, to deal with downsizing initiatives, allowing people to start moving towards retirement and take an amount of reduced work time but continue to pay into their pension plan at full rate, creating other opportunities and development and training for employees, both current and new workforce. According to HR3, 'management accountants play a major role in providing the various aspects and concepts for accounting to the decision-makers because this is a huge financial impact on the corporation'.

MA4, at the divisional level, explained that one of the roles of MA at the division is to provide the elements of added value, balancing HR business strategies with business issues, at the same time creating a business environment by providing elements of a clear link between corporate strategy and business strategy. For example, to increase market share of the business, management accountants provide information for decision-making and building business strategies in achieving both business and corporate goals.

Analysis and setting targets

The other area where the issue of MA contribution was identified was in providing analysis at different stages of the HR strategies. MA1 expressed strong views about her role in contributing analytical factors that would provide opportunities for market growth and further play a facilitating role in setting up business strategies to integrate those opportunities.

HR4 indicated that he provided financial analysis on employee training and development, 'our group do all types of financial analysis related to HR', and gave an example: 'how our budget is set up for training and development, can we handle the training programme, how many people are we going to send to our training, we look at the ratio, development costs, is it cost-effective, does that make sense ..., so those kind of analyses'. HR4 further elaborated, 'one of the big challenges I have is to bring financial discipline into the HR community'.

MA2 supported his role in providing analytical work for operational strategies and by preparing business cases for major projects: 'We would prepare a business case and take it forward, if it requires funding, if it's something we can do within our budget then we would just do it. So we would prepare a cost–benefit analysis, what we are going to do, what it costs, what are the benefits and the overall impact.'

During the strategic planning process, MA4 has a team of six members (directors) with different disciplinary backgrounds and supports senior executives to make strategic decisions: 'We try to provide the process around it and to provide a lot of the research, we do a lot of the competitive analysis, market analysis and financial/non-financial analysis, all that information is very critical for our high-level strategic planning.'

Performance measurements and reporting

MA1 gave a broader perspective on the MA contribution to business growth:

> to provide mail services to all of Canada and obviously to sustain the company in terms of long-term growth and in order to do that with shrinking letter mail, letter mail is a good percentage of our business, but with the Internet and all the other nice electronics, pay by mail, pay via bank. There is a shrinking business here. But there are lots of opportunities on the electronic side for us as well – this is where finance comes in.

The MA contribution in expanding markets includes implementing commission, a compensation plan for sales people linking it to HRPDP strategy, tracking revenue and setting targets for sales people.

HR4 has responsibility for the complete HR community. In explaining his role, HR4 said, 'Basically, if you slice my responsibilities into components, I have planning, accounting or financial support, analysis and reporting of the HR functions or the HR group.' HR4 also expressed the view that there is a relationship between HR and finance, for example in measuring performance. Further, the measurements are compared with plan or target, compared between other regions and also benchmarked with other companies: 'For instance, we compare how much we spend on training against other organisations, benchmarking internally, establishing a target and seeing how close we are to the target and also comparing with last year.' The CPC is very labour–intensive, with a rapidly increasing cost of benefits. According to HR4 the cost of benefits six years ago was 15 per cent, in 1999 it was 21.7 per cent and the forecast is around 25 per cent in the near future. There are other labour costs, such as absenteeism rates, turnover rates, hiring costs and cost of benefits, which are all critical and have a big impact on the bottom line. This is where the HR and finance groups work together to provide these financial and non-financial measures that are important in decision-making.

According to MA4, his contribution is also supporting the implementation process: 'Finance itself does not exist, it is an integrated role. Too many finance people are trying to figure out what happened yesterday. In theory we would like to spend 60 per cent of our time on new development, evaluation of business cases.'

HR4, having a finance background, takes a dynamic role creating links between HR and corporate communities and also between the HR resources, performance and strategic goals. In reality, HR4 is performing a function of MA in an attempt to provide performance outcomes of HR strategies in terms of productivity, employee turnover, absence rates or accidents, and attaching financial values to the benefits. Further, in this case, management accountants are a part of the HR community and have a close relationship and clear communication with it, and provide the fundamental guidance needed to ensure the success of the HR policies, procedures and strategies. Management accountants contribute in communicating information in a language that is easily understood by the user. MA2 said, 'there is a real interest in what is behind all these numbers and I think my area of finance probably has a bit of a communicational role – a bit of a teaching role'.

HR3 summarised MA participation in the management process right from planning to reporting:

> at the beginning of the year when we set our budgets, we work with the finance group a lot, they have to understand what we are doing, so they play a key role there, but they play a key role one step before that which is the preparation of the HR strategies, so it starts off with the strategic planning, then based on that plan, the preparation of the budgets, so that's number two, they are involved in budget preparation. And then after that it's the monitoring, we meet occasionally every two months to review and monitor. Then the next road is the reporting, they help us to develop some measurements that are meaningful, financials and others. We are developing the HR scorecard now for HR and the financial group are participating in that development because there are obviously some numerical measurements that have to be done, but they also understand there are non-financials. Finally, we have to develop business cases, and again they help us, they help us right through the steps.

Seven respondents (MA1, MA2, HR3, MA4, US2, HR3 and HR4) identified different aspects of the MA contribution with respect to performance measurements, including setting targets, performance indicators – both financial and non-financial – measuring those targets and comparing with budgets and analysing the difference where needed.

HR3 underlined the importance of human resources: 'Our labour costs are 65–70 per cent, very high, and when you think of it, what's your biggest asset? It's our people and it has to be number one and human resources are an integral contributor to the corporation's success.' HR3 elaborated further by explaining the process of establishing HR strategies and their measurements: 'Canada Post is putting into place now a formal HR scorecard, a scorecard that can tell the Management Executive Committee and ourselves, how do we contribute to the bottom line.' The key point he mentioned was that finance people are working very closely with HR and his group to develop a formal professional business scorecard for HR measurements: 'Finance contribution is that they help us measure the HR scorecard, manage our budgets, control our spending and control our costs and help us prepare business cases.'

MA4 brought up an interesting performance measurement concept with respect to a strategy initiated by Canada Post called the Double Diamond Production System. The idea behind this strategy is to become more efficient in its delivery time and deliver essentially a better-quality product and reduce internal waste in the process. In order to measure the efficiency of the system, it needed to set the target for cost efficiency and 'initiate the process of understanding what has to be the performance measurements that will drive the behaviour that we want to find on the floors'. Working as a team, including the finance group, they came up with financial and non-financial measurements, 'things like cost and resources involved, cost per piece and cycle time [the time taken from the time the product was picked up to the time the product was delivered] to measure the efficiency'.

4.5 Summary

The CPC issued its Human Resources Direction for 1998/99, which gives highlights of the HR strategies and their importance. Human resources are an integral contributor to the CPC's success by increasing customer satisfaction through employee satisfaction by:

- developing leaders that demonstrate behaviour consistent with the Leadership Profile;
- developing programmes that recruit, retain, develop and reward employees to ensure the right people at the right time with the right skills;
- creating and promoting an environment that moves responsibility for people management to those who manage people;
- integrating and aligning HR strategies with functional business strategies;
- establishing effective communication to ensure that the Human Resources Direction is achieved and maintained;
- establishing a value-added continuous learning environment to ensure employment and employability;
- creating a climate of respect, trust and co-operation between management, employees and unions.

HR3 summarised the strategy objectives: 'The purpose of all of these strategies is to improve the bottom line. It is proven that there is a direct link between employee satisfaction and customer satisfaction. We also know that there is a link between customer satisfaction and customer loyalty. And we know there is a link between customer loyalty and profit.' By creating innovative HR strategies, with continuous training and development (HRPDP), developing management programmes (MOSDP), driving towards leadership, teamwork and people management–management behaviour (CPC Leadership Profile), and finally acknowledging the contribution made by each and every employee (Employee Recognition Program), the creativity and knowledge of the workforce is enhanced, which in turn creates the foundation that strengthens the links with their customers. In creating that foundation, MA plays a major role in the domain of the HR strategic management process.

One of the priorities set by CPC is to push for more decentralisation, to ensure that decisions are taken at the lowest possible level, where the effects are felt immediately. With this priority in mind, the strategic planning process developed by CPC is an integrative approach. The role of MA in relation to the HR strategic planning process is both at the lowest level, where specific strategies are initiated and developed, and also at the corporate level, where broader strategies are presented and approved, in which MA plays a major part. Further MA contributions in the HR strategic management process are in providing analysis, setting targets and measuring performance. The above contributions not only enhance the quality of the decision-making process, but management accountants are a 'business partner' and also take part in decision-making. Figure 4.6 illustrates the CPC's key HR strategies and the contribution from MA.

Figure 4.6 Canada Post Corporation's key human resource strategies and management accounting

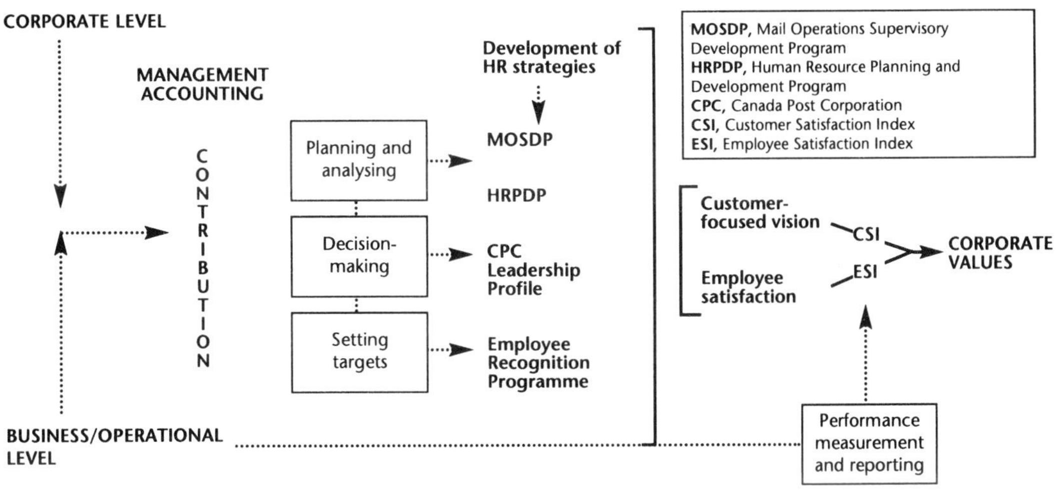

The Corporation has taken an integrative approach where the contribution is made from both the corporate level and the operational/business level in developing HR strategies for the management/leadership/supervisory skills training and development programme. Having a clear vision of the objectives to contribute to corporate values, management has focused on customer and employee satisfaction. In the process of developing these HR strategies with the above focus, management accountants played a part at both corporate and business level in planning, analysing, making decisions and setting targets for these HR strategies. For example, what needs to be done in providing superior management skills, individual needs, improving interpersonal skills, support and quality of service to satisfy both employees and customers? Analysis of the resources available includes financial resources. What are our targets? How are we going to measure these? Further, management accountants played a key part in performance measures and reporting at both business level and corporate level.

One of the questions posed to all the respondents was to give their views on the future role of MA in relation to HRM. MA4 provided his views by commencing with MA's current role:

> The role today is more of data gatherers, preparing reports and keepers of the binders that are filed and never looked at. The role in the future, probably more of a partner role with the people on the floor, not only making sure the information gathered is analysed and understood, but also provide the indicators, for example cycle time – non-financial measures, the dashboard – sort of assessment risk to make intelligent calls on a real-time basis.

According to HR3, HRM and MA are integrated partners:

> We do have some people in HR that have a sound financial background and we do have finance people that have some HR background; one thing which

would be nice is to allow more exchange between the two functions, and what I hope would be for finance people to understand HR even better. We know specialisation is important, but it is better to understand each other's job because we can help each other. Finally, it is definitely a partnership role and an exchange role and helping each other to achieve the same goal, after all, we are all aiming for the same thing.

MA4 explained the MA future role from his perspective:

> I see the finance folks to be much more involved in the customer value proposition, we as finance people have unique skills and understanding about costs, cost structure, cost drivers and so on. When you want to create value you got to be able to put together business proposals. Further, finance people could report numbers which is one thing but I think commenting and interpreting the meaning of the numbers are more useful – looking forward.

MA2 gave his views on the future role for management accountants as providing and taking part in decision-making and advice-giving.

What HR3 would like to see MA providing are key indicators on HR strategies:

> give us good feedback on how we are doing, key indictors that will say these programmes are effective, these programmes are achieving what they were intended to do, and I think there is a big role to be played by MA.

In order to achieve common goals, the future role of MA, according to HR4, is for management accountants to understand the business operation and for HR people to understand the finance discipline.

Finally, MA1, Finance Director, elaborated on the future role of MA:

> Well, what we are evolving here is to become more of a business partner with the upbringing community and so the evolution here has been rapid over the last ten years. Ten years ago when I started, what Finance did is, it produced some numbers, put them into a package, sent it off to the General Manager, and he'd take a quick flip through the numbers until the next month and then would do the same thing all over again. Now, what you find is the finance is a key player on the management team within Western Canada and we are evolving to a point where we are the advice-givers, not only from the point of view of the numbers but in terms of strategy and that sort of thing. It's been a long haul to get us from those guys in Finance to here but what we are doing is as a team. But we are there. Are we 100 per cent there yet? No. But we are way down the track now from where we were. It's been an exciting development in evolution over the past ten years. There are no decisions made that don't touch me in some way in Western Canada.

5

Case Study No. 3: TDG plc

5.1 Research site

5.1.1 Overview

The research site for this case study is a large UK-based transportation company. The company, TDG plc, is a leading European logistics group operating throughout the UK and other major Western European countries. The group's Board of Directors consists of the Non-executive Chairman, the Chief Executive, three Executive Directors and three further Non-Executive Directors. Day-to-day operational control is managed by the Management Committee. The members of the committee are the Finance Director, the Human Resources Director, the Chief Executive and the other executive director. The group employs over 80,000 employees throughout their operations in both the UK and European countries.

5.1.2 Business details

During 1998, as a result of the company's strategic review, the core activities were reorganised under two broad segments: (1) packed product, and (2) bulk activities – henceforth referred to as KDM Grouping and SGB Grouping respectively. Each of these groupings is managed by the Board Director. The management structure is shown in Figure 5.1.

The businesses under KDM Grouping within the UK are primarily those of TDG Beck & Pollitzer, TDG Harris and TDG Williams. Each operates in defined market areas evolved to reflect a new customer-focused divisional structure within TDG. As part of the Industrial Division, the company provides logistics services to customers within the industrial and manufacturing sectors. The SGB Grouping is structured under three operations: (1) Ambient Storage, (2) temperature-controlled storage known as Cold Storage, with operations principally in the UK and Ireland, and (3) Bulk Logistics. Ambient Storage is able to offer a vast choice of ambient warehousing in a number of different locations within the UK, using the operating names TDG Data Storage and TDG Pinnacle.

TDG owns and operates cold storage operations in the UK (under the name of TDG Novacold), and in Ireland (called Autozero Ltd) and also on the European mainland. The TDG Novacold cold storage business provides services to a large span of industry that requires term storage and management of moving product flows. There are 32 units in the UK alone, offering more widespread coverage than any other company.

Figure 5.1 Management structure of TDG plc

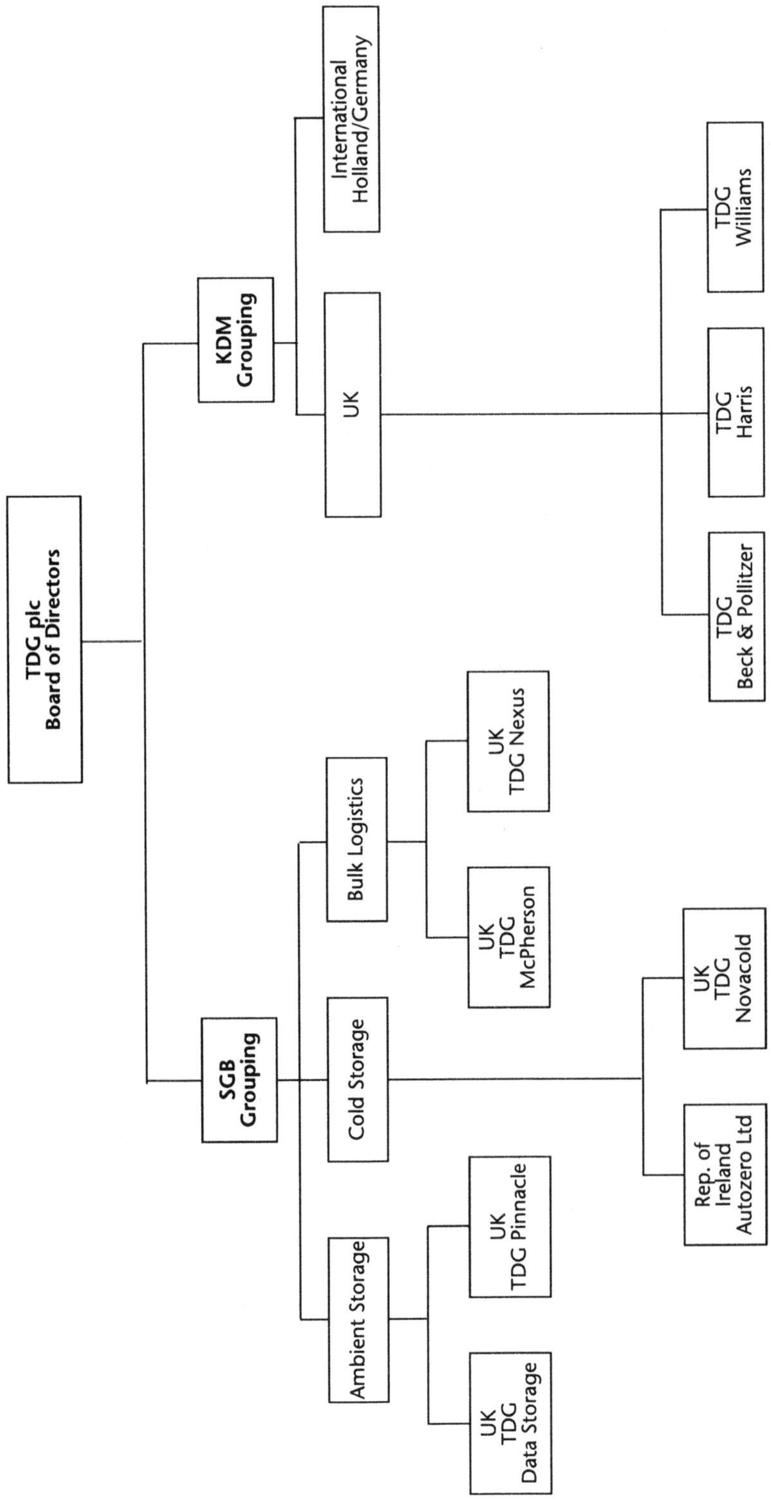

The SGB Grouping operates its Bulk Logistics Division through TDG Nexus and TDG McPherson. The focus of its tanker operations is on the chemicals, petroleum products and alcohol sectors. The packed product logistics activities of KDM Grouping has operations in UK, the Benelux countries, France and Spain. These activities are area-focused on the following sectors: automotive, chemicals, DIY, drinks, electronics, fast-moving consumer goods, food, packaging and paper.

Each business unit is decentralised with profit centres and has its own business structure with functional areas and respective directors. These directors, for example, HR Director, Finance Director and Operational Director, have reporting responsibilities to TDG's Managing Director. By grouping packed product, logistics activities would allow further efficiencies and cost reductions and create opportunities for profitable growth.

Regarding the UK bulk tanker and storage businesses, the reorganisation would provide opportunities to widen operations to encompass more value-added areas such as plant services and repacking. The storage activities have prospects of adding further sites once all the cold stores have been fully integrated.

TDG has other businesses that are outside these core activities and are of low growth potential. For example, TDG Vehicle Rental was sold during 1997. Currently TDG owns and maintains over a fleet of over 4500 vehicles to the highest standards, which is renewed in a continuous programme of reinvestment. The group has its own modern service facilities for the maintenance of its vehicles around the country and in addition utilises Freight Transport Association engineers to carry out spot checks.

- *Business information systems.* TDG has started a project to centralise all of its financial processing to yield better-quality and more meaningful management information. The company's investment in information technology is critical in improving efficiency for corporate growth. According to one manager, the new information system is a crucial factor in implementing the business strategy. The company is currently installing new financial processing software, which is being introduced at the same time as sites are being networked with new desktop computers. The new systems are millennium-compliant and the capital cost of these investments for the future is estimated at £6.25m, to be written off over the next five years. The implementation of these new systems was completed during May 1998 and progressively rolled out during 1998. The final sites went live on 1 January 1999. Over 1000 staff were trained to use the new financial system based on the JD Edwards software.

- *Financial overview.* The group turnover is £500m and the group has conservative accounting policies, owns most of its premises, and has strong cash flow, modest gearing and a strong balance sheet. Sales grew to £529.1m in 1997, an overall increase of 1.4 per cent over the previous year. Operating profit after interest increased by 4.2 per cent to £35m on a turnover of £529m, up from £522m in 1996. Earnings per share on this basis have risen by 11 per cent as a result of this increase and the December 1996 shares buy-back. In August the company released the interim results for 1998. Operating profit, before interest, for the first half of the year was £18.4m against £16.3m the previous year. Operating profit for 1997 was higher than in 1996. The growth was the result of continued development of logistics activities and good performance in storage and UK tanker businesses.

5.2 Primary data

5.2.1 The interviews

The interviews were conducted at various sites and varied in length, with an average of about an hour. Half a day was spent touring a Novacold storage facility, one of the sites of the company. The Operational Manager during the tour gave an overview of the Novacold storage facility, and reports pertaining to that specific site were obtained. Over the following two weeks a total of eleven respondents were interviewed. Notes were taken in the interviews, recording of the interviews was later transcribed and formats of reports were obtained. Notes were also used during the coding process. The following respondents were interviewed:

1. Group Finance Director (MA).
2. Group Human Resources Director (HR).
3. Operational Manager (US) – Harris.
4. Finance Director (MA) – Harris.
5. Personnel Director (HR).
6. Human Resources Director (HR) – Nexus.
7. Finance Director (MA) – Nexus.
8. Finance Director (MA) – Pinnacle.
9. Divisional Operational Director (US) – Brewing Operation.
10. Divisional Operational Director (US) – Manufacturing, Hatfield.
11. Information Systems Manager (US).

The above respondents' profile references are used in the following sections.

5.2.2 Secondary data

Annual reports, organisational charts and other business reports were obtained from various sites visited.

5.3 Results

In this section categories of issues of importance to the respondents are presented. The label given to each category is grouped into strategies and each group of strategies is presented in the following section.

5.3.1 *Business strategy*

The company is operating in a growing market for the outsourcing of logistics and the group's key strategy is to win a good share of that growth. The company's focus is to concentrate on core logistics-related markets that have the highest potential for future growth, and to become the first-choice European logistics supplier to the industrial and manufacturing markets by the year 2000. The company's strategy for growth has been well communicated to all business units and operations. The business units' strategies are developed to achieve the group's strategy for growth. HR2 indicated, 'our business strategies are linked through the Managing Director, his key role is to interface between this business unit and the group strategy'.

5.3.2 *Part A: Human resource strategies*

The company is aware that in an increasingly sophisticated and competitive environment its ability to improve efficiency and offer maximum cost-effectiveness to its customers will be by gained primarily through the commitment and dedication of its employees.

According to US1, 'the focus is to ensure that we provide the customers with the service that they are paying for and we achieve that at a cost which is acceptable to the customers'. US3 mentioned that for their business operation, the growth is to improve services for existing accounts, expand those existing accounts and develop new business. Therefore, it is very important to establish a relationship and develop credibility with customers: 'understanding and having in-depth knowledge of the business is very critical'.

HR2 pointed out that 'strategic planning is done at the board level and at the business unit level we establish objectives and plans to meet the demand of that situation while striving to reach the organisation's objectives'. HR2 identified the business units' perspective: 'business strategy for this business unit is about developing strategy in terms of where the business is going as a combined entity'. The HR part of that strategy is what people or employees can do to help support the strategy. HR2 further explained that in the contract industry such as this, there is inevitable legislation surrounding transport undertakings, giving a high-profile role for HR to play; the HR Director is therefore involved with the business development along with other business directors in order to move towards the achievement of business strategy.

The business strategy at TDG Harris is to improve operational standards on existing sites and to increase market share in non-food retail areas. Within TDG Harris a strategy called Harris Hallmarks has been developed, which is aimed at delivering an overall strategy of cultural change that is linked to business growth. US1 pointed out that 'the key issue for us is that we are trying to develop a new culture within Harris. This new culture supports the company's strategy for future growth'.

US1 explained that the role of Managing Director of TDG Harris is to make sure that the business strategies are in line with the TDG group strategy: 'We are putting more detail around the broad corporate strategy, for example, the broad corporate strategy for Harris is to grow in retail and food manufacturing and it is our business strategy to develop tactics on how we are going to achieve business growth.'

According to US1, the cornerstone of Harris Hallmarks is the way they want employees to focus on customer requirements and have effective and regular contact with the customers. At TDG Harris they have developed a strategy to ensure that methodical processes are adopted and maintained. The procedures are documented, reviewed and regularly audited; for example, all employees need to have clear job descriptions specifying individual responsibilities. They also have a strategy of teams acting together effectively, and enjoying the work by open and honest management style, encouraging innovation and enabling individual progress within the company. Clear induction, training and development programmes are established. There is training for teams to be accountable for high standards of health and safety, cleanliness and security.

Further, at Harris it is important, according to US1, that in order for the company to increase its market share, employees need to be fully aware of the markets in which it operates by providing management and staff with regular information on company performance, customer progress and market trends. In addition, training programmes are necessary to refresh knowledge of relevant techniques and technological innovations. With an increase in market share, the emphasis is also on cost improvement. All activities are scrutinised for value and market competitiveness.

The above key focus points can be achieved by people development, according to US1. He further explained that, in order to achieve the overall business strategy, they need to focus on people: 'It is not about knowledge and skills but about behaviour and we are looking at seven key elements or key characteristics and this is what we call people strategy.' The elements he was referring to are for employees to learn and develop techniques to manage their own behaviour, for example, develop self-control and ability to cope with pressure. They want employees to drive for achievement to challenge the status quo, pushing for continuous improvement with concern for quality, focus on achievement, having systematic judgement of opportunity and evaluation of a situation to understand and make things happen. One of the characteristics US1 mentioned was to have wider vision, aware of the wider business context of the business by understanding the business environment and the marketplace. Finally, there are the interpersonal skills, understanding customers, their needs and expectations, and to be a team player.

Therefore, the emphasis has been placed on HR strategies by investing in people ('Investors In People', a government-sponsored programme) through training and development including management skills, technical skills, driver training, agency training, safety and communication. For example, TDG Beck & Pollitzer has developed a framework for effectively communicating the business objectives to its employees and gaining their commitment to achieving the objectives. US1 pointed out that communication to employees is the key to developing the overall strategy: 'I get together with my people as often as I can and talk about how the business is going, what our operational issues are and get them involved in getting their input in development of issues, this is all part of trying to develop one team.'

'Investors in People' provided the business with the opportunity to develop a skilled workforce where employees are well informed, and confident that their contribution to the success of the business is valued. Setting objectives for training and development followed by evaluation ensures that the training budget is well spent and provides the business and the customers with efficiency and value for money.

Training and development

At TDG Tanker, the business unit's strategic objective is to improve profitability and increase market share, with emphasis towards value-added services; for example, repacking products rather than just a straightforward system of taking tankers from one place to another. In order to achieve this strategy, according to MA1, 'providing proper training can enhance quality service and get closer to and understand a customer's production process'. HR3 explained how important this strategy is:

> this business is all about winning and losing contracts and therefore you are always winning and losing staff but we have got to create a culture and provide them an environment which contributes to the profitability of the company. This strategy is about retaining staff and motivating employees. For the overall strategy of growth under the umbrella of TDG, one thing the business unit can do is through the medium of training, where we are trying to change the culture, the one vehicle to work is the vehicle of training.

This training includes senior management training, a training centre to look at health and safety and driver training. Integrated training is also provided for business unit depot managers to break down the barriers and create opportunities to interact and interface with other depot managers.

Third-party (Oxford Training) training modules are also being used in the development centre. Currently at the business level, the training started with depot managers 'to establish trained leaders so that our management team is in place, but we also have other basic skills training and training programmes like training to operate a forklift. We have basic supervisory training to develop basic people skills.' Training and development is designed at the business unit to suit the needs of the business unit; for example, at Nexus, besides the driver training, there is technical skills training for the employees on an ongoing basis.

US3 identified management training at his business unit which is based on annual appraisal for each person working at that business unit. Once training needs are identified, these individuals are not only given basic-need training, but the issue of safety is emphasised.

The company also has a management training programme. For graduates, the core of the external management training programme is the one-week introduction to management course. This provides an insight into the main management areas and into TDG, as well as providing an opportunity for graduates to meet their contemporaries from other TDG business units. In addition, many graduates take advantage of the training opportunities set out in the TDG internal programme to meet specific job requirement skills, knowledge, and attitudes to take on responsibilities.

One of the business units (Nexus) won the 'Investors In People' award, and HR2 identified the importance of training: 'We have a process of identifying and flagging our training needs and that leads to some sort of demand that helps individuals think about their training needs and that helps push demand up a bit.'

At Nexus, according to HR2, an employee survey was conducted after the implementation of 'Investors in People' and found need for improvement in the communication of business objectives and plans. Another survey was planned, related to safety, to get feedback on best protective equipment, best training and other safety issues. Further, MA1 commented on special training in health and safety to carry particular products.

TDG has won more industry awards in recent years than others for training its staff and has also won its fair share of customer service awards. In the fields of safety and environmental responsibility, the group sets standards that are advised internationally. TDG Harris, for example, holds the British Safety Council Five Star Award, and TDG Beck & Pollitzer achieved the world's first BS 7750 environmental standard award.

Driver training

The strategy of driver training has shown a significant impact on the bottom line. For example, the emphasis on safety through training has meant that the number of accidents has been reduced drastically and thereby significantly reduced insurance premiums.

HR3 mentioned, 'HR is about recruiting the right people, remunerating the right people and retaining the right people and therefore our HR strategy is focused on training. Training is cultural change, gives us a far more efficient, better-educated company with far fewer industrial tribunals, far fewer staff leaving, far better trained than we ever were, and thereby winning more business than we ever did.' HR3 commented, 'driver training is very critical at all business units, specially at one of their tanker businesses'. According to MA1:

> we make sure our drivers are properly trained, these drivers go through 'Five Star Training' and are monitored constantly by giving them feedback on both positive and negative outcomes. These drivers carrying hazardous products are trained on how to handle those products safely. There is also training on fuel consumption, as fuel is their big variable cost. There is also basic standard health and safety training.

HR2 commented on training where there is heaviest spending – driver training: 'it is a driver training programme and the strategy was adopted by the group. Each driver must go through this programme.' US3 explained that the key people strategy at their business unit is driver training. The policy for driver training is developed by the TDG Group, called the Five Star Drivers' Training programme, at each business unit. The programme allows each driver to go through an intensive training programme.

Because of the nature of the TDG business, a very significant part of the total costs for TDG is drivers' labour cost. Therefore the key strategy for business units is a first-class driver training programme. This has an impact on the bottom line, and is measured by the number of accidents and the insurance costs.

MA1 explained that the training strategy at business units is tied into group strategy:

> we identify what sort of markets we are trying to get into. We know we should identify particular skill shortage within business units and try plugging those gaps. For example, we are trying to get further into the production process, where the added value bit comes in, this is where our people are trained properly to understand the customers' business.

Driver training sessions were modified to improve drivers' skills and improve fuel conservation through the use of better driving techniques. According to US3, they also provide all the other training necessary to develop skills like forklift truck driving training; training is provided to warehousemen, and safety training is also one of their top priorities. During 1997 the company successfully completed an in-house 'TDG Driver of the Year' competition, in which a full range of skills was examined. In 1997 the UK accident frequency rate was down 12 per cent compared with the previous year. Further reductions in prohibitions and convictions were also achieved.

Agency driver training

Risk analysis techniques provide a focus for the group's efforts. For example, statistics compiled by TDG have shown that agency drivers, utilised to cover peak periods of business, experience almost twice the accident rate of TDG's own employee drivers. In response, TDG established a mandatory policy during the year to ensure that, before operating a TDG vehicle, agency drivers demonstrate satisfactory driving standards to the group's qualified assessors. US3 explained that if they use agency drivers, these drivers have to go through an assessment centre and all agency drivers must meet basic standards before they are employed. HR3 mentioned that every one of their agency drivers now has to go through quite a severe driver training test just to be an agency driver with them.

Safety

Safety continues to be of the highest priority for the company. In 1995, the Board set up the Vehicle Safety Committee in recognition of the importance of safety to the group. The management committee laid out the following objectives:

- to encourage the development of a safety culture in all vehicle operations;
- to ensure the safe and legal operation of all group vehicles;
- to ensure that all drivers are being trained to a common, consistent and high standard;
- to monitor and review the group's accident statistics and maintain standards.

HR3 pointed out that the driver training and safety policy led the industry. The safety policy includes a programme of external audit of vehicle maintenance that not only ensures high standards and reduced costs, but has also been a factor in winning business from safety-conscious customers.

All TDG drivers of large goods vehicles receive at least one day's training annually in 'safe and economical driving' techniques. In addition to the driver training programme, a variety of means are employed to raise vehicle safety awareness. During 1997, these included the successful in-house 'TDG Driver of the Year' competition, in which a full range of skills was examined, and the co-production of a safety video, which was released industry-wide in collaboration with the Vehicle Inspectorate.

The group's initiatives to improve safety awareness and performance within its operations continue to yield encouraging results. As mentioned earlier, in 1997 the UK accident frequency rate was down 12 per cent on the previous year and, based on independent inspections carried out by the Freight Transport Association, vehicle defects were half that of the industry as a whole. Further reductions in prohibitions and convictions were also achieved. One of the TDG sites holds the British Safety Council Five Star Award as well as the Council's prestigious Sword of Honour. Individual operations within the businesses are subject to audits by the Health and Safety Executive to ensure that standards do not slip.

5.3.3 Part B: Management accounting contribution

Part B represents the MA contribution in relation to the above strategies. The primary objective of the reorganisation of the management structure for TDG is to increase profitability of the company in the logistics competitive market and enhance shareholders' value. One of the key members of the Board and also the Management Committee is the Finance Director. Therefore, the Finance Director plays a role at the strategic level in planning, decision-making, and analysing performance. There is an important contribution from a management accountant as a management committee member in setting up policies and procedures, including policies on the HR side. According to US3, 'business strategies and employee hiring is done at the business unit level but following the central policies and procedures'. On the MA role in relation to HR decisions, MA2 commented, 'Well, I am currently involved in the salary scheme and also review the training programme and look at vehicle safety and the accident records. I have the Insurance Department reporting to me so I get functionally involved in that aspect of the HR side.' Further, 'I would express my views on contracts when the Chief Executive may need a second opinion on certain contracts, but there is a finance director reporting to the business unit who is more experienced understanding the detail of these contracts than I am, so the Finance Director and the business unit make sure the financials are right before any contracts are sent out to customers.'

One of the biggest problems the company was facing in preparing consolidated financial and non-financial reports was because of the underdeveloped information system. MA1 stated: 'When you try and get to the situation of interfacing between the accounting systems of business operations, at the moment they are not integrated.' The company is in the process of upgrading the entire system, where financial reports for all business units can easily be consolidated. According to MA2, 'with the new system, we will able to produce all management information which can easily be analysed for decision-making'. At TDG one of the outstanding contributions from MA is the development of an information system for the entire company. MA2 not only initiated the project for an effective, efficient and more meaningful management information system, but was also a key player in the entire management process of the new information technology. For example, MA2 had a key role in the development and implementation of the system, making sure that the system not only met the needs of corporate reporting, but also all the sites' and customers' requirements. MA contribution also included hiring internal (information system manager) and external (professional consultants) key personnel to make sure that the project is carried out successfully.

One of the broad strategies mentioned by HR1 at one of the operating sites was in terms of business developments, where a team of people were working on tenders or contracts. One of the members of this team is a management accountant preparing the financial part of the contract for the whole project: 'Those numbers obviously include the labour costs, and so either directly or as part of the team process, I contribute by feeding numbers into the process, making sure that the whole proposition is properly costed. I work with the management accountant and the financial controller on issues like redundancy pay, loyalty payment costs, placement costs and so on.' He further said that his role

> is a business role not as the welfare function. I actually get involved with operation directors on the day-to-day operation of the business, so I am an operations person whose specialism is in human resources and I think that is what HR should be. I seek to develop my people in those areas.

HR1 expressed his views regarding performance measurement on HR strategies that it is difficult to quantify because the focus of their strategies is preventative: 'Training people to do disciplinary procedures correctly prevents *x* number of industry tribunals. How many? It is impossible to quantify. So much of our work is preventative, the other thing is if you are training people to be better at what they do how do you actually quantify that? It is quite difficult.' But he further explained that they do look at other outputs that are directly or indirectly the results of their strategies, 'where we can measure and I make a point of measuring is we had a £100,000 refund from the centre on our insurance bill because the number of accidents were down. Why were the number of accidents down, because we did a "Five Star Training Programme". The impact is straight on the bottom line, so it is possible to quantify those situations.' Furthermore, all business units maintain systems enabling training results to be monitored and display statistics relating to vehicle safety, accidents and fuel performance.

At TDG Harris the productivity is measured by establishing key performance indicators. For example, it has established standards of performance in terms of how long it takes to pack a case, movements of trucks, and labour hours in terms of cases per attended hour. It also does benchmarking with other sites to find an improved way of achieving better performance. The other measures are, according to US1, 'we measure the percentage of the utilisation of the vehicle both in terms of number of hours and the truck or vehicle loads. It is important for us to know the effectiveness of how we use them.'

The above key performance measures are collated by administrative people and at some major sites the information is compiled by management accountants. US3 commented that some of the most important key performance indicators are number of accidents, labour costs, number of loads per employee and driver training costs. These performance indicators are centrally co-ordinated by an operational management team, not management accounting.

At TDG Harris the overall strategy is retail and food manufacturing growth and, according to US1 the broad strategy of growth can be achieved by working through people. So at a business level, the site has developed detailed Harris Hallmarks for people development in order to achieve business growth. But what role does MA play in this HR strategy? US1 replied, referring to their Finance Director, 'our Finance Director is definitely part of the entire process. He is part of the team that developed strategy, and he plays a part in the development centre. Our finance team has to be part of the overall team and understand the strategy and be able to say, well, this is taking us forward.'

Management accountants provide information in terms of period reporting and financial reporting and 'they have a key contribution in the area of cost-effectiveness and are part of the project team in producing the costs and understanding the customer's strategy and they are involved in the development as well as ongoing operations'. US1 further stated: 'to do my job, finance group is an essential part of the review processing in terms of our operations. Management accountants are an important part of our business development team and their contribution in analysing the operations' issues helps depot managers make the right decisions'. According to HR3, the HR Director determines the salary structure and group bonus schemes. The salary information, annualised hours, and any other people costs for all business units, are drawn through the centre by accessing all the business units. This information is provided by the business unit personnel group. These people costs are also captured by management accountants and built into the monthly financial reports. Further, HR3 mentioned that the budget part of the people costs is provided by Human Resources and then integrated into business plans.

HR3 also mentioned agency costs, where the business unit would hire outside employees on a temporary basis. These agency costs are compiled by the business unit personnel group on a daily, weekly and monthly basis and consolidated by the HR group. The agency cost information is critical in preparing the contracts. For example, HR3 explained that it is cheaper to have permanent drivers than agency drivers. Therefore, information on the cost of agency drivers, number of accidents, accident statistics, training of drivers, recruitment, and any other people costs, are critical in decision-making. However, this information, provided in monthly reports on what is happening at the business units, is provided by personnel managers. So what role does MA play in providing information? HR3 commented, 'Well, I see the financial information at the monthly management committee and MA provide information in decision-making; for example, if we are losing money at one of our business units, then, we would analyse the situation and my contribution would be personnel issues.' He further expressed his views on the role of MA: 'I have sufficient information gathered by personnel managers for me to make HR decisions.'

MA1 expressed his role as an integrated one, in managing people within the business unit, all aspects of financial functions including forecasting, budgeting, cash management and also 'spending fair amount of time at the depot with the operations interacting with operation directors and also human resource directors'. Further, he explained that in the process of preparing budgets all people costs, like training and direct labour costs, are put together by the HR group, but management accountants integrate with other disciplines to get information and put together financial and budget package: 'management accountants are part of the teams taking an active part in discussing different issues like operational, HR, safety, customer and other issues brought up in the meeting'.

According to MA1, management accountants provide key performance benchmarking with other business units, for example, the training costs across the business units. MA plays a different role at different business units with TDG, because of the different type and size of the business units. For example, according to US2, the role of management accountants is to support contract managers and their team. As for providing information on HR issues, US2 commented, 'we have our own people costs including overtime and agency costs. Management accountants contribute analytical information, which is critical for operational decisions, for example is it cheaper to have employees work overtime or hire agency employees?' Further, US2 continued, 'we do various analyses and we sit down with the management accountants to produce the budget and we look at some of the "what ifs", for example, what if we only work two or three shifts, and what would be the financial impact of that? We also look at annualised hours where management accountants would be involved in simulating that process.'

US3 explained:

> Our strategy is to improve productivity and working with the customer to become a more integrated operation so that customer sees us not just as a contractor, but part of their operation. And that's probably why I spend so much time with our customers because I want the customers to see us being a tool who can bring them benefits. To provide customer benefits, our employees have to work as a team, if you don't have the right people to operate then we are not moving towards effectiveness. So it's people, it's the investment in people that counts and it is very critical for our management team including management accountants to understand customers and their business.

According to US2, management accountants contribute by working with the team of depot managers in developing models of annual budget planning and analyse the actual performance with budget: 'measuring performance is an integral part of financial reporting, we have accountants monitor costs against the forecast. This is where management accountants play a role in monitoring and policing.'

In preparing the annual budget, according to US3, management accountants would get involved with depot managers, operational directors and HR directors: 'As a team we would discuss the issues to be built into the budget. We look at various elements and key performance indicators, for example labour costs, number of loads, mileage and volume delivered. So in order for management accountants to prepare the entire budget package, they need to understand the business aspect of it.' Management accountants do the actual preparation of putting the budget together.

At the manufacturing business unit, the people costs, the productivity of their drivers, the number of loads by each driver per day, and various non-financial performance measures are important for the Operational Director; however, according to US3, this sort of information is compiled by the operational management team: 'Our contribution from a management accounting point of view for the entire operating division is on a non-financial basis.'

The tanker business is very much a contracts business where HR, the Business Development Director and the Managing Director would get involved and visit customer sites in gathering information for preparing contracts. As for management accountants' involvement, HR2 said:

> our Finance Director would sometimes get involved depending on the size of the contract. If it was a smaller contract, then we would get one of the sites operations accountants who supports the operation and commercial people in the same way that I do on the HR side. Management accountants help contribute by doing the analysis necessary for the development of the contracts and high-profile role for HR to play in providing information about employee issues.

Further, HR2 mentioned that a lot of HR-related information such as safety data, accident incidents, analysis of labour turnover and absences would be provided by the site administrator, depending on the size of the site.

5.4 Summary

The summary of this case study is illustrated in Figure 5.2, which shows the HR strategies developed from the group's strategy for growth that is developed through the strategic planning process by the Board and Management Committee. The figure also shows the role MA plays at different stages of the HR strategies.

From the corporate strategy, business units have developed and established key HR strategies to meet the strategy for growth and achieve business units' objectives by focusing on employees and customers. The emphasis of the key HR strategies was placed on training and development, including technical skills, management and supervisory skills, driver training, agency training and safety. Investing in employees ('Investors in People') by training and development providing increased skills, knowledge, ability and motivating employees through open communication and building teams to improve customer service, and to increase the logistics market and profitability.

Figure 5.2 TDG's key human resource strategies and management accounting contribution

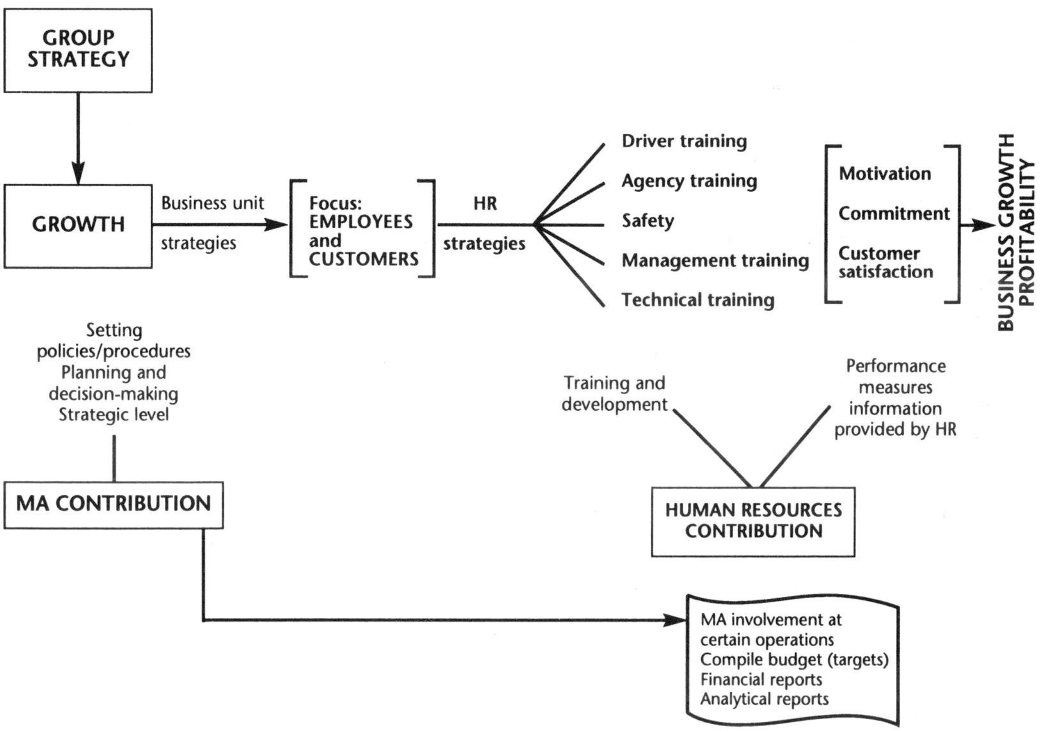

The TDG group is committed to a policy of offering career development opportunities to its staff, and spends around £2m annually on training. Typically, 90 per cent of the group's UK workforce attend programmes each year, covering a wide range of subjects. TDG's dynamic personnel policies have been recognised by the Institute of Logistics with the prestigious award for Excellence in the Field of Human Resources. MA involvement is clearly seen at the strategic level in planning, decision-making and also contributing to the decision-making process, monitoring and providing analytical reports. The role of MA is stated differently at different sites. At certain business units, management accountants are heavily involved at the operational level as members of the operational management team, whereas at some locations, management accountants just provide monthly financial reports, a basic financial function.

At certain sites, managers gather and analyse budget information in consultation with site managers. Management accountants basically use the model developed by the depot manager and help prepare the annual budget. Again, the budget is presented to internal management by the depot manager and any changes are forwarded to MA. In this respect, management accountants' contribution is limited with regard to getting involved with other managers and gathering and/or analysing the budget numbers.

At other sites management accountants were involved from the initial stage of the budget preparation all the way to analysing and making necessary changes, in addition to monitoring the actual performance measures against the budget targets, and contributing to controlling and providing information in making decisions at all the levels of strategy. US2 expressed his views on the consultative role of MA at their operational site: 'We have regular discussion with management accountants together with senior people from site. We also look at the development of ideas as we go towards the budget process. So there is very much involvement from management accountants in all aspects for our business.'

Overall, managers believed that the future role of MA is to provide more analytical, 'what ifs' and for management accountants to get involved at the operational level to understand the operational aspects of the business in order to achieve greater participation in providing information at the decision level. One of the managers pointed out that it is important not only to understand the logistics business of the company, but it is also critical for management accountants to understand the customer's business.

As for the future role of MA, HR1 mentioned that MA and HR management work on each other's territories and it is important that both are business managers rather than just being in specialised areas:

> I think for management accountants to be more business managers than financial managers. In the same way that I strive to be a business manager who specialised in HR, they should be business managers that specialise in finance because then they have the breadth to be able to balance off the way the operations managers have to balance off. Further, management accountants need to take a broad and long-term perspective on all business aspects.

He explained the above by giving an example where MA helped save £300,000 by applying a financial judgement from a business perspective, 'I think almost in any function of any sort of support service, if you have that breadth you can double your impact. They are not just accountants but more business managers because they do understand our business.'

One of the outstanding roles played by management accountants (MA2) is in visiting different sites on a regular basis, understanding the operational side of the businesses, having meetings with key personnel at different sites, understanding their problems and concerns and contributing in the development of the business. Further, for the future role of MA, US1 expressed his views:

> I think the role is about interpretation and evaluation of things rather than production of numbers. It's interpretation and providing people like me with the best advice about those numbers and be a part of the overall business and also new business development.

According to MA1, the future role of MA is to be able to understand the entire operation in order to provide meaningful information:

> I think it's certainly becoming clearer to me that we need to be providing more general accounting support to the operational side of the business and get more involved in the lower levels of the operations so we understand the numbers better and bring some sort of financial bent. Today, management accountants need to understand operations otherwise we end up failing the operations.

US4 expressed his view on the future role of MA:

> I think management accountants need to support their operational colleagues. So far management accountants have provided a role in this business of generating numbers to a set formula, a set pattern once a month, maybe weekly reports, maybe those in need of contracts. Well, certainly those numbers do not provide analytical perspective and more specifically I think they probably provide less information for new contracts or new business development. Getting involved at the operational level and understanding the operation side of the business would provide better information in business growth.

US2 gave his version of the future role of MA as providing 'what ifs' analysis:

> the role of management accounting would be to provide the service to support the operation. For our business, we have different customers, so I need to develop models to look at 'what ifs' and what adds value to the operation. Further, to improve performance, the major tool of management accounting would be working with operation managers/directors like human resources and be a team player.

MA4 identified another important MA activity as the breakdown of costs into constituent activities. This provides an opportunity for greater understanding of an operation and for bringing about changes to activities as necessary. By incorporating both financial and non-financial information, MA can provide more insight for managers and directors than information provided by financial accounting alone. US3 commented:

> What I would like to see is MA giving me a detailed breakdown on key performance indicators and reasons behind that would include the operational understanding. I am getting the information but there is a lot more management accountants can do if they understand the business not only on a day-to-day basis or what has gone in the past but in developing new business to look forward, and therefore I would like MA get more involved at the operational level.

Even though HR has its own role to play, HR3 would like to see finance and human resources in more of an integrated role:

> HR function generally over the last ten years has changed significantly because it used to be very administrative. Now HR need to interact and interface very closely across the channel, management accountants need to know what industrial tribunals are going on, what the union problems are, what the wage demand problems are and quite obviously what has an impact on the performance of the business.

6

Case Study No. 4: Weycan

6.1 Research site

6.1.1 Overview

The primary research site is one of the pulp divisions of a Canadian forest company (henceforth referred to as Weycan), a wholly-owned subsidiary of a US company (henceforth referred to as Weyco). The principal businesses are the growing and harvesting of trees; the manufacture, distribution and sale of forest products, including logs, wood chips, building products, pulp, paper and packaging products; and real estate construction and development. The company is also one of North America's largest producers of forest products and a leading recycler of office waste paper, newspaper and corrugated boxes. Weyco employs 45,000 employees, with 4800 employees in the Canadian operations.

Weycan's businesses are categorised into three major segments: (1) pulp, paper and packaging; (2) solid wood, timberlands, and (3) sales and distribution. Figure 6.1 shows these three major business segments and their subcategories by geographical location. These operations are located in British Columbia (BC), Alberta and Saskatchewan. The BC pulp mill, which is the research site for this case study, is indicated by an asterisk in Figure 6.1. The chart also shows the key functional areas of the BC pulp mill under the direction of the Vice President and General Manager, BC Division.

6.1.2 Organisation

Weycan began operations in 1965, growing to become one of the largest forest products companies in Western Canada based on sales and assets. Canadian operations account for a significant share of the US company's North American activities. Canadian manufacturing represents about 17 per cent of all the company's pulp and paper products, 34 per cent of all softwood lumber output and 58 per cent of oriented strand board (compressed finished wood) capacity. The following gives a summary of Weycan's operations.

The Canadian operations produce a range of pulp, paper, lumber and engineered panel products for Canadian and international markets. The company operates six sawmills in BC's southern interior, three sawmills in Alberta and one in Saskatchewan. Combined annual capacity of all sawmills exceeds 1 billion board feet. It employs 1400 people. Lumber products include North American Construction and appearance grades, J-grade for Japan, and machine-stress rated and performance-rated

Figure 6.1 Weycan Canadian operations and BC Pulp Division organisation chart

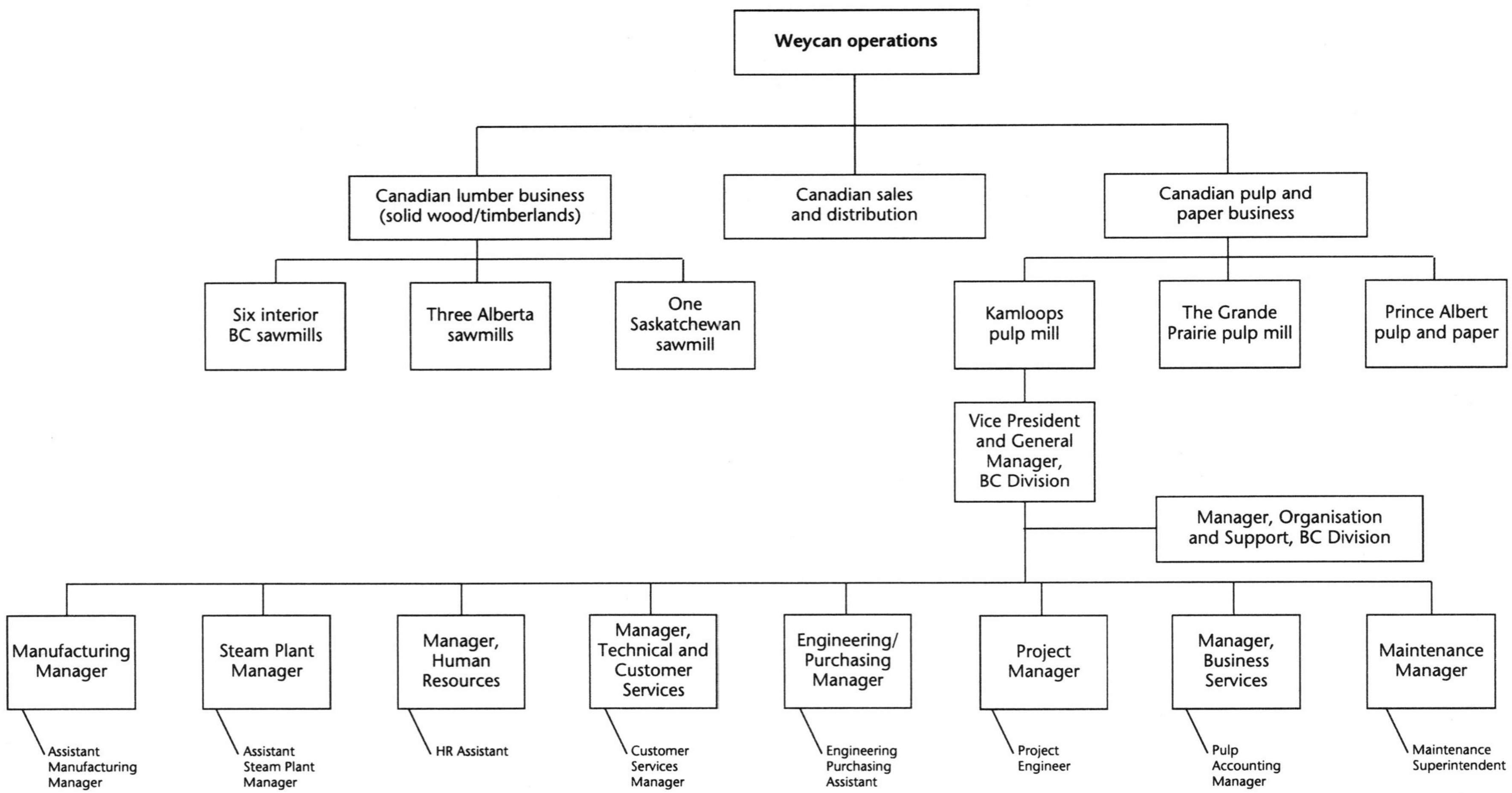

lumber for the truss industry. Canadian Lumber also operates a major trading centre in Kamloops for the distribution of its products.

Engineered panel products – Sturdi-Wood, an engineered oriented strand board product using aspen fibre – is manufactured at three processing facilities in Alberta: Drayton Valley, Edson and Slave Lake. The combined capacity of these mills exceeds 800 million ft^2 (3/8-inch basis) annually. Sturdi-Wood is marketed in Canada, the USA and overseas. The business is based in Edmonton and employs about 550 people.

Building Material Sales and Distribution is a network of seven Canadian customer service centres and eight sales offices and reload centres across Canada. These sales and distribution centres provide sales, marketing and logistics services to lumber dealers and home improvement warehouses. About 20 per cent of Weycan's solid wood production are sold in the Canadian market, with the balance exported to the USA and overseas.

The Grande Prairie, one of the Canadian pulp mills, began operating in 1973 and was acquired in 1992. It produces softwood bleached kraft pulp. Pulp from the mill is marketed primarily in the USA for use in products ranging from quality writing paper to paper towels. The mill employs 500 people. Current product capacity is approximately 300 tonnes a year. The pulp mill located in Prince Albert began operations in 1968, processing softwood pulp and adding hardwood fibre in the 1980s. Weycan acquired it in 1986. A fine-paper mill, completed in 1988, includes both cut-size and folio paper-sheeting machines. Primary uses of the paper products include business forms, photocopier paper and commercial printing stocks, with major markets in the US Midwest and Canada. Prince Albert Pulp and Paper employs 850 people. Current annual production capacity is approximately 160 tonnes of bleached kraft pulp and 230 tonnes of uncoated free-sheet paper.

6.1.3 Pulp Division business details

The BC pulp mill was built in 1964 and began its operation in 1965. Through expansion and upgrading, the mill has become recognised as one of the finest world-scale, internationally competitive mills in North America. It produces three grades of bleached and semi-bleached softwood kraft pulp. The fibre supply for the pulp mill is drawn from sawmill residues. Wood chips, sawdust, planer savings and hog fuel are supplied by six company sawmills and by 20 independent sawmills within a 200km radius of the site. The BC pulp mill operation has 600 employees, including the administration staff.

- *The operation.* Current production capacity is approximately 450 tonnes a year. Within the pulp mill there are two mills: Mill A produces 'Tyee' kraft bleached kraft market pulp from mill residuals such as planer shavings, screened sawdust and pin chips; Mill B produces 'Kamloops' kraft bleached kraft market pulp from residual chips from area lumber mills. Pulp grades produced at Kamloops are named after indigenous fish: the Kamloops trout and the Tyee salmon.
- *Financial overview.* The weakness of several international economies and the slow recovery of worldwide pulp prices resulted in a price of $1.76 per share, a fall in Weyco's share price from $2.34 per share in 1996 to $1.96 in 1999.

Because of efforts to continually improve the operations, the company fared better in 1997 than it would have otherwise done in an industry downturn of this magnitude.

Since 1992 the company's return on net assets (RONA) has ranked in the top quartile, and total shareholder return has ranked second among the 13 companies it tracks as a peer group. The company's internal research and external analysts indicate that RONA is the strongest driver of shareholder value for the forest products industry.

HR2 briefly reported the financial outcome: 'The fact is, we were pleased to report that last year we were the number one forest products company in the world in terms of return on investment. That's the good news, the bad news is we were 7.9 per cent RONA and the big challenge of forest products companies in business in general is to try to increase that RONA, and our new target is 17 per cent RONA.'

6.2 Primary data

6.2.1 The interviews

The interviews were conducted at the Pulp Division and also at the head office located in Kamloops, BC over a two-week period. A total of eleven interviews were conducted, with an average duration of just over one hour. All the interviews were conducted at the mill site, with one exception. This interview, with the Vice President, Human Resources, was conducted at the corporate head office. Notes were taken during the interviews and tape recordings of the interviews were later transcribed. The profile of the respondents is as follows:

1. Superintendent, Employee Relations (HR).
2. Vice President, Human Resource (HR).
3. Pulp Accounting Manager (MA).
4. Manager, Organisational Development and Support (HR).
5. Engineering/Purchasing Manager (US).
6. Manager, Business Services (MA).
7. Customer Service Manager (US).
8. Steam Plant Manager (US).
9. Manufacturing Manager (US).
10. Manager, Human Resources (HR).
11. Day Superintendent (US).

6.2.2 Secondary data

A pulp mill tour was undertaken and collection of other secondary data were collected with regard to organisational structure, company vision, values, principles and corporate strategies, together with company-wide aspects, including the HR strategic focus and detailed HR and MA reports.

6.3 Policies and strategies

HR2 gave an overview of the strategic process of HR strategies: 'Human resource strategies start with our vision as a company, our values and our business strategies. We do have this concept of one company with respect to vision, values and strategies, so that's where it all starts and that is the glue that holds us all together as one company.'

Weycan is seen as part of Weyco and considered as one company that ties into Weyco's vision, values and strategies. HR2 explained: 'Divisional strategies and values don't change from year to year, what does change is the company-wide areas of emphasis.' According to HR2 the HR strategies are developed from the corporate strategies and areas of emphasis.

The senior management who set the direction across the business develop the vision, values and strategies. According to HR2, the senior management team 'is sending a message to all senior leaders of the company that the focus areas are safety, competitive leadership around earnings and processes, process reliability, work system improvement and diversity'. The business units across the company have developed strategies and improvement plans linking to the above five areas of emphasis set by senior management. With respect to these areas of emphasis, HR2 commented, 'from Human Resources point of view, safety, work systems improvement and diversity are all directly related to people management'.

The company also uses councils to bring about an improvement in HR management within the company. HR2 explained: 'Ultimately, the businesses own their human resources strategies but we are using councils in the United States as well as in Canada.' The members of each Human Resource Council are a representative from (1) Pulp, Paper and Packaging Division, (2) Wood Products, (3) Timberlands and Distribution, (4) Labour Relations, (5) Corporate Employee Relations, (6) Corporate Human Resources, (7) Weyco Executive Vice President of Human Resources, and (8) Weycan Vice President of Human Resources. According to HR2, 'the HR council is a sort of a cross-section of senior HR people across the company and they come together and their role is to provide leadership to strategic areas of the HR focus'.

The role of this HR council is to provide leadership to strategic areas of HR focus, provide leadership/counsel to the senior management team and sponsor HR function priorities. According to HR2, 'the Human Resource Council is set up to develop standardised processes where it makes sense and basically work together on how we can synergistically work together to improve the bottom line'. The HR Council provides leadership in key areas in HR management and in the 1998 HR strategic focus areas. The HR Council also provides the assessment tools and process support. According to HR2, linking action plans and tactics to company-wide areas of emphasis and developing strategies are done at the business level, 'so this is a sort of micro of what we are going to do as an HR Council in 1998'.

On the Canadian side there is also a management team known as Corporate Managers Team which plays a key role in establishing the company's strategies linked to the organisation's vision, values and strategies. This management team is chaired by the President of the company. HR2 added: 'and to enhance shareholder return in a manner consistent with the company's vision and values. The team is uniquely positioned to provide leadership in seven broad strategic areas, Forest Land, Business Synergy and Integration, People Systems, External Affairs, Market Intelligence and Growth Opportunities, Legal and Regulatory Compliance, and Board of Directors'.

HR1 stated: 'people here are not involved at the initiation stage but most of the people at the mill level here are involved in implementing those strategies'. These strategies at the mill are developed by a site Leadership Team whose members are, according to HR3,

> Manufacturing Manager, Steam Plant Manager, Technical and Customer Service Manager, Business Service Manager [financial manager], Organisation and Development Manager, Human Resources Manager and Maintenance Manager; basically, all the managers at the mill level directly reporting to Vice President and General Manager, BC Division [see Figure 6.1] and a management accountant.

HR3 explained the strategic process at the mill level:

> We take the vision, drive out the objectives, look externally and internally, figure out what the big hitters are for us at the mill from the external scan, revisit a definition of our objectives and desired future state, talk about major issues affecting us at this mill level and talk about five-year business plans integrating strategies.

6.4 Results

This section presents the primary data obtained by interviews and documents collected at the research site. The abbreviations introduced in the profile section above will be used here to identify individual comments.

6.4.1 Part A: Human resource strategies

The corporate head office located in the USA (Tacoma) has identified overall five key target areas of emphasis. Figure 6.2 shows the flow of HR strategies from corporate vision, values and strategies, as explained by HR2. These areas of emphasis are developed from corporate strategies linked to corporate vision, 'to be the best Forest Product Company in the world, and values "Customers, People, Accountability, Citizenship and Financial Responsibility"'.

Figure 6.2 Human resources strategies linking to corporate vision and values

CORPORATE VISION

'The Best Forest Products Company in the World'

CORPORATE VALUES →

- Customers
- People
- Accountability
- Citizenship
- Financial responsibility

Corporate strategies	1998 Areas of emphasis	1998 HR strategic focus
Making total quality the way of doing business	1. SAFETY	Safety
Empowering people	2. COMPETITIVE LEADERSHIP	Leadership development
Producing superior returns for shareholders	3. PROCESS RELIABILITY	Customer focus
Relentless pursuit of full customer satisfaction	4. WORK SYSTEMS IMPROVEMENT	Work systems improvement Labour principles/partnerships
Leading the industry in forest management and manufacturing excellence	5. DIVERSITY	Diversity

Work Systems Improvement strategy

Based on the areas of emphasis set by the senior corporate executives, the business unit has developed the Work Systems Improvement (WSI) strategy, which is one of the key areas of the 1998/2000 HR strategic focus. Seven respondents (HR1, HR2, HR3, MA2, US4, HR4 and US5) made comments about the WSI strategy that relates to people, customers and accountability, which is part of the organisation's core values.

HR2 explained that 'the WSI strategy is a business-driven goal and the company is working towards a healthy work system incorporating all of the principles'. HR2 gave a small card that listed the following principles:

1. Full customer satisfaction.
2. Involving everybody in the organisation.
3. Respecting and developing people.
4. A safe, clean, orderly workplace.
5. Company-wide customer–vendor accountabilities.
6. Developing and using reliable methods.
7. Managing with facts and data.
8. Continuous improvement.
9. Eliminate all waste.
10. Management controls focusing on goals and means.

HR2 further explained that the ultimate objectives of the WSI strategy is 'to lead to better results in productivity, profitability, customer service, quality, safety and to develop work systems that fit today's people, technology and business'.

HR3 reported that the 'Work Systems Improvement means redesigning the work. It is a means to better business performance by employee involvement, commitment, flexibility and ownership.'

HR4 elaborated on the strategy: 'The organisation needs to empower people by increasing their knowledge and understanding of the businesses in which they're engaged and the work processes they manage. Also by developing all levels of competency, in all areas of technical, business, interpersonal, improvement and self-management. Further, give authority to people to act to satisfy customers.'

HR1 explained that the activities for WSI strategy have already been implemented and 'we are basically in the first year of this work systems strategy which is really looking at fundamentally changing the way we do work here, changing how we utilise people more efficiently'. HR1 explained that work system change is 'getting people out of the "sandbox" mentality, knock down the sandbox and begin to do other things that I am very capable of doing, so we got to get rid off this rigidity, less dependent upon direct immediate supervision, less reliant on immediate direction guidance, be more flexible and it starts with management'.

According to HR2, the company is in the process of providing multi-skills to the HR community through a number of different training and development courses: 'we have a three-week course on change agents and champions, we have got an annual work innovation study and exchange conference within the company'. The bottom line of the work systems change strategy is to make sure people are given more opportunities to make their own decisions, and given empowerment, continuous improvement and flexibility. They are also looking at a soft version of HRM; they want people to be committed and feel good about them (MA1).

US4 expressed his thoughts on the work systems strategy from the operational perspective:

> The work systems improvement is Human Resources strategy which is already implemented and we are working how to better utilise the people at work here and, you know, we have been handicapped to some extent by fairly rigid work rules and a unionised workforce for a number of years and that might be changing somewhat now, so what we need to take advantage of this strategy.

US4 stated: 'We are expecting our employees to utilise more skills that they haven't utilised to date, and we also need to train them with some skills that they don't have if we expect them to be more flexible.'

The strategy of work systems change is to reduce the pulp manufacturing costs through flexibility and other initiatives such as being adaptive and receptive to innovations (US4). HR4 stressed the importance of flexibility and empowerment that would have an impact on the bottom line: 'in order to survive, we are looking at having flexibility and work systems change, from management's perspective, the goals are to have more productivity, better customer service and improve quality'. The strategy of WSI creates those activities that add value, which is what the customer wants, and that is customer focus.

According to HR4, they would like to see full flexibility for the workforce, which means that all their employees will utilise all their current skills to do work that they have traditionally not done and, in addition, to train the entire workforce again to acquire news skills. He said, 'the ultimate objective is for this mill to survive'. This was supported by US5; according to him, the work systems strategy is 'to improve productivity, flexibility and acquire multi-skills to be able to work to their capabilities rather to the restrictions to their given trait'.

As for the target and measurements, HR2 stressed, 'the CEO of the company a couple years ago said that by the year 2000, every unit will have made substantial progress in terms of performance and the bottom line'. As explained by HR2, the outcome of the strategy is, 'we have experience in our company that says a high-involvement work system will generate anywhere between sort of 20 to 30 per cent bottom-line improvement just by virtue of the work systems'. HR2 summarised the concept of the WSI strategy, as shown in Figure 6.3.

Figure 6.3 The Work Systems Improvement strategy

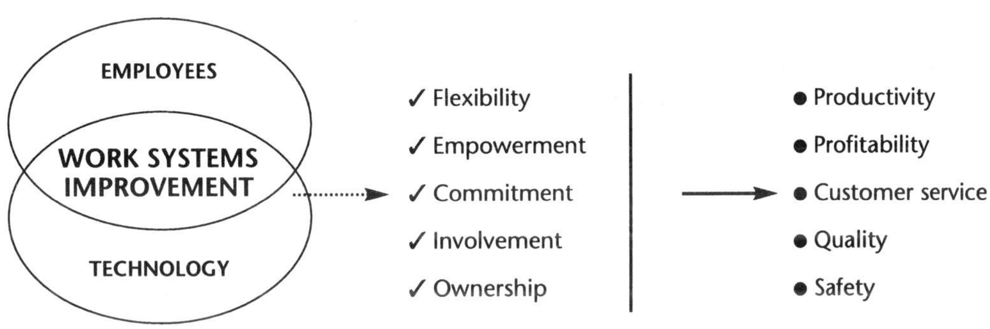

Weycan Leadership Education strategy

The Weycan Leadership Education (WLE) strategy emphasises educating leaders and developing leadership qualities. According to HR4, the objective of the WLE 'is to have all of the Weycan leaders headed in the right direction in the future'. The outcome of the WLE training is to get all their leaders across the organisation thinking the same and understanding what the companys' vision, values and strategies are. According to HR2, leadership involves creating a vision of the future, devising a strategy for achieving that vision and communicating the vision so that everyone understands and believes in it. The focus of the strategy is an influence process that involves communicating corporate objectives and motivating leaders in pursuit of those objectives. Leadership education is one way of developing a system necessary to support its strategies.

HR3 explained, 'with the focus on leadership training, we have now a week-long education session designed by the HR3 team communicating concepts on corporate vision, values, involving training and development on work system and leadership education to improve leadership behaviour to work towards common objectives' (Figure 6.4). HR1 explained, 'the goal is to establish an educational package for leadership'. The emphasis of this strategy is 'to communicate the corporate vision, enhance visionary leaders to make the vision happen'. According to HR4, they have already gone through the pilot session with the senior leaders: 'the corporate managers have committed their time to this education and without their commitments we cannot take it all the way down to first-line supervisors'. HR4 explained the importance of the strategy: 'the company approach to leadership to achieve its mission is by having committed leaders'.

After the first pilot session, HR4 stated, 'it was very worth spending my time there and that it showed to me that the company is committed in preparing their leaders to move into the future and there are a lot of good tools that leaders can use in their respective roles'.

US5 mentioned that he has facilitated some of the leadership training sessions. The leadership training modules are developed internally and the trainees are leaders of different disciplines. He explained that he was very pleased with the areas that were presented:

> It is a significant strategy for Weycan and is really targeted at the front-line supervisors, but it applies to all management people who have a role in directing and leading people and is targeted in helping leaders understand what the plans are, what the company's vision, values and strategies are and what they can do to help achieve those plans.

Figure 6.4 The Weycan Leadership Education strategy

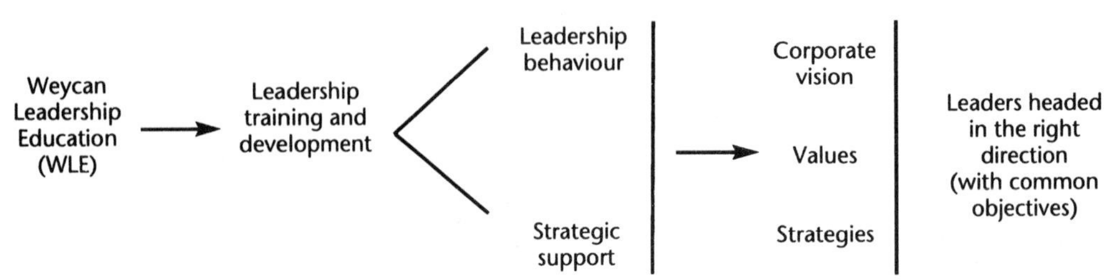

Diversity

The strategy for diversity is to balance the workforce profile. The organisation has developed a strategy called Diversity because, as quoted by HR2, 'a highly diverse workforce is a competitive advantage'. According to HR2, 'it's good business to value diversity of people and ideas and to respect the capabilities of all employees'.

Human resource management expressed the view that, 'we must recruit and retain the best people, and to do so we must focus on creating a climate where a diversity of people and their innovative ideas are valued'. In their workforce profile the focus is to continue to work on goals for women and minorities in management and professional positions. The company-wide 1998 targets for placements are as follows:

	Women	Minorities
Managers	32%	12%
Professionals	40%	13%

To achieve acceptable company-wide progress, HR2 claimed, they need to understand the root causes. They have established a procedure to analyse the barriers to achieving the goals or targets for placing women and minorities in management and professional positions, and report results and recommendations.

HR2 said, 'management desire to have a company to reflect the communities in which we operate and also reflects our customer base and we believe that there is a real business advantage'. The strategy for diversity 'is *not* a source of weakness, it is a source of strength'.

Health and safety

One of the key areas of the corporate values focuses on people (employees), and states that 'our success depends upon high-performing people working together in a safe and healthy workplace where diversity, development and teamwork are valued and recognized' (according to the Weyco corporate document). In line with these core values, HR1 suggested, 'the core value that the company has is to provide a healthy and safe work environment and in order to fulfil that value it is imperative that every mill has a comprehensive health and safety plan'.

Safety, which is the division's number one priority and is to be the top priority in every operating unit, was commented on by four respondents (HR1, HR2, HR3, and US3). The company indicated a strong interest in moving towards behaviour-based safety approaches where each individual learns to take an active role in increasing his or her safety and the safety of others. Selected processes are currently being piloted under the guidance of the Safety and Health Council. Key learning and processes are implemented more broadly in 1998. HR2 commented, 'we are striving for industry leadership in safety on the pathway to "world-class" performance'.

Their 1998 target is a recordable incident rate (RIR) of 3.0, which translates into a company-wide target of 35 per cent improvement over the 1997 target. In line with the target, one of the key points mentioned was that they are shifting the emphasis to RIR because the safety triangle ratios show a direct relationship between fatalities and serious injuries and the number of recordable and lost-time incidents. There are also other non-financial measurable targets used by the division, for example, lost workday rate. The progress on the targets is reported at quarterly business reviews. HR2 pointed out that understanding the root causes of incidents should reduce incident rates and severity and should lead to the elimination of fatalities. According to HR1, 'The overall goal is to have zero accidents, and to demonstrate that our number one priority and one of the core values is the healthy and safe workplace.'

According to US3, 'every staff member has to have a special safety project. Either an employee performs a safety presentation for the Steam Plant for training and development or they have an external safety expert come in and do some training. We also have regular safety meetings where we share ideas on safety issues.' With regard to safety, US3 explained that they also have environment training and environmental policies that all tie into the mill safety policy, which is specific to this mill.

6.4.2 Part B: Management accounting contribution

This section discusses the role of MA in relation to the HR strategic process. At Weycan Pulp Mill, the Finance Manager plays an integrating role in the process of developing, planning, analysing, contributing to decision-making, measuring performance, monitoring and controlling in relation to HR strategies.

The Finance Manager, a key member of the leadership team at the pulp mill, plays a major role from the stage of the corporate objectives to the development of HR strategies at the mill level; for example, his role in contributing procedures and policies for a safe and clean workplace, helping to develop reliable methods, ways of eliminating waste and focusing on continuous improvements. His contribution is in providing information about the skills and training needed to improve safety. Having knowledge about the business and the operational aspects, the Finance Manager regularly attends the safety meeting and, if there are any accidents reported, he plays a role in analysing such accidents and provides suggestions for improvements. According to MA2, there is a contribution from management accountants in setting up procedures to help achieve safety targets. Further, management accountants contribute in analysing leadership training and development and provide information to help plan the leadership training. For example, the company recently went through the leadership training seminars for all supervisors; the Finance Manager helped to plan and budget the entire training process and at the same time contributed in controlling activities and monitoring the amount spent on training. In some areas he also made suggestions for developing modules for leadership training.

According to the Finance Manager, understanding the inside of these HR strategies gives him the strength to contribute in analysing, monitoring and reporting the outcomes, and that makes it easier for him to provide recommendations for improvements. With regard to HR functional areas, management accountants do play a small role in recruiting the best people by being members of the hiring committee, depending on the position to be filled. The Finance Manager's professionalism provides powerful and positive thoughts in the decision-making process that, according to him, has an impact on the company's strategy for diversity.

One of the key performance measures or indicators that the company looks at very critically is RONA. This measure among other reports is prepared and presented by management accountants during their monthly mill meetings. Further, any changes to RONA or the bottom line is explained by management accountants in detail. According to the Finance Manager, sometimes the change is because of some of these HR activities or strategies being implemented, for example, maintenance shutdown, or major employee training, or negotiation on major safety issues. This is where management accountants get involved in contributing the critical information, which explains the bottom impact, based on these HR activities.

The above are some of the examples that the Finance Manager provided in linking HR strategies and the contribution made by management accounting.

According to MA2 there were two reasons why he played an integrating role. First, he is very business-oriented, and second, he has been with the company for a number of years and understands all aspects of the entire operation of the facility. MA2 commented, 'basically, as a finance manager, my role is to support the vision and values to provide the leadership'. MA1 further explained what the role of MA is at this mill level: 'the role of MA is not to tell the management why we cannot do something but in fact help them find a way to do it'.

HR2 pointed out that it was critical to have financial people as members of their corporate management team: 'our financial manager is one of the key members of our leadership team, he is not just wearing a financial hat, but he is truly a business-contributing member of the team and so he brings financial perspectives but also contributes to all aspects of business'.

A similar comment was made by HR3:

> The financial manager wears different hats, he understands the whole business not just the numbers, and so he adds value in discussions that are not purely in his functional area. So, for example, we had a meeting yesterday about principle-based leadership and the financial manager added some very good perspectives on how we should go about doing that and help us bind to our principles.

Further, he added, 'the financial manager adds value because having a clear understanding of the business without having to use the number side of his head when he sits in the room, he adds value in that perspective'.

According to HR3, before they finalise any targets it is very critical that those targets are passed through the MA group to get their views, comments and suggestions. HR3 explained:

> In all these objectives and targets, there are probably 25 of them. Ten of them we wouldn't touch without having good financial depth behind it. Financial Manager and his group provide kind of the 'core' work. They support those production planning, cost planning, fibre cost management, these are some of the core things that we could not work effectively without having a financial manager. The ten targets and objectives I mentioned above, the other fifteen we could live without the financial manager's input, but we wouldn't because, for two reasons, one, for example, we are talking about taking an additional month of downtime because of pulp market and doing a whole bunch of work systems, work with our employees' training, involvement, that kind of stuff. The financial manager's contribution is the cost, the downstream and so on. My second point on these other fifteen is having the business understanding is important no matter what you are talking about, and that has impact on our targets.

Finally he stated, 'to add to the answers I have given, the contribution from the Financial Manager is an absolute must, we would not function very well without a financial manager and it is important that they be at that level as part of our team'.

HR4 expressed his views on the MA contribution: 'Our Financial Manager is part of our leadership team and he contributes like all the other managers to the work system plan.' He further explained how MA played a role in ensuring that the information provided was easily understood by the people at the mill level: 'We have a very strong financial group here with good people who add a lot to the organisation with respect to reporting and analysing the data.'

HR2 explained one of the roles of MA: 'Certainly, the financial people would be heavily involved in this whole area of competitive leadership and business improvement plans to increase return. I guess one area where the financial community and the HR group overlap is in this people-soft implementation and as I look at our focus areas here the financial people would *not* get involved in labour relations principles.'

HR3 commented, 'it's the Leadership Team who reports to Vice President and General Manager, BC Division, and these are the managers, including financial people and all the managers like manufacturing and technicians. This management team within this division would provide all the relevant information with respect to actual performance measures which are then compared with targets to monitor the progress towards the strategies.' According to HR3, the role played by the financial manager is very critical at all levels: 'he [the Financial Manager] has been part of the team all the way from the corporate level all the way down starting from the organisational vision coming up with objectives and strategies'.

Even though the strategy procedure is top-down, the strategic process at this mill level is different, in a sense that 'there are different cultures, the president of the company does not know the culture of every single mill but he does know that as an overall guideline this is where we want to go. That is what he has established. Our job at the mill level is to take that and say how does that apply to us, what can we do to achieve those corporate objectives, and that is the part we at the mill leadership team have to do.'

According to HR3, the WSI strategy is an HRM model that leads to a high-performance workplace, 'there is a link between WSI and firm profit', and MA plays a vital role in providing information on performance. The HRM strategy's focus is on improved performance – this means greater attention is given to financial target-setting and performance-monitoring. One of the key measures used by the company is RONA for comparison with competitors. The financial group provides this information. HR3 stressed that this measurement is very critical, as some of the strategies developed are based on where the company stands compared with a similar industry; for example, quality enhancement, cost reduction and improved productivity. This is where MA provides critical information in making high-level decisions.

There is a direct link between corporate strategies, with HRM strategies and corporate vision and values to achieve the corporate vision. According to HR2, the key performance indicators compiled by the Finance Manager and his group are reported at their leadership team meeting because those indicators are used to assess the progress on the business plans and strategies. In addition to the MA contribution in providing targets and performance measurements, according to HR3, with respect to the WLE strategy, a management accountant played the role of a *trainee* once he has been trained and gone through the leadership training process.

Management accountants provide analytical information and also participate in the decision-making process (MA2). MA2 expressed his views on the decision-making process: 'My contribution has an impact on how all decisions are made at this mill and through the Vice President and General Manager, his contribution is how the mill business is going to be run and then his boss has the contribution to how the pulp and paper sector is being managed.'

According to HR3, 'there are some parts of the plan where without the financial manager's analysis and inputs, we would not make good decisions'. At the operational level, US1 mentioned that when a new project is initiated they form a team and someone from the MA group is a member of that project team, right from the start contributing to aspects of the project: 'Their [management accountants'] contribution is key in making the right decisions to get the project off the ground. Further, the analysis of information provided on a regular basis helps us in monitoring the projects to make sure we are on the right track.'

Management accountants provide analytical support at different levels and areas in the strategic process (MA2). MA2 explained his contribution: 'My function is to participate in the leadership team that supports the mill and provide the analytical support.' He further explained, 'I don't spend a lot of time doing the accounting, I spend most of my time on the management side. At corporate level, my role is to understand the business, what it means, what we have to do and take it down to the next level.'

Planning for a major project, MA provides analytical information for decision-making. MA2 gave a broad view on his role as an analyst: 'I support on the analytical side, and also where the opportunities are through educating the workforce so that they understand the key leverage points at the mill and what the impact on the bottom line is by the actions and decisions taken at the operational level.'

Management accountants also contribute in relation to non-financial performance indicators with respect to health and safety strategy. Management accountants compile information on the number of accidents, days off and accident rates. Management accounting plays a role in providing performance measures, both financial and non-financial, not only for the senior management team but also for line workers, in a language that is easily understood by them. The senior management does a monthly briefing and the information is compiled by the financial group. During the monthly performance briefing meeting, management accountants also participate in answering questions from operational people and help them understand about cost management.

HR3 commented that, at the business unit level, 'mill performance is analysed when developing strategies which are linked to areas of emphasis identified by the senior management. Therefore, in developing strategies, management accountants participate in performing various analyses, for example, financial resource and profitability.'

Behind every strategy there is a certain expectation of results and there are targets. For this mill a comment was made by HR1 regarding the target costs of pulp per tonne. This target is the mill's break-even measurement, which is provided by MA. Therefore it is very important, according to HR1, to understand what the target amount is composed of, in order to improve productivity, quality and profitability.

The contribution from the financial group from the operational point of view is in providing statistical and non-financial information. US4 gave an example: 'They provide chemical usage and production statistics and quality statistics.' He further pointed out:

> Financial people give us some daily and some weekly and some monthly reports and so we get data and we need this data in order to manage our business. Now we have gotten more data electronically and through mill-wide information systems than we have had in the past. But we still rely on the statistical information, sort of summary in a concise form that we can take action on awfully quickly and this information is provided by financial people.

Further, he explained that management accountants participate in safety meetings and provide information on non-financial safety measures; for example, one of the key measures for safety is the RIR, which they compare with the company-wide target and monitor the improvements compared with previous years.

US4 expressed his views on how important the performance measurements are. According to him, performance measures and targets are developed to support business objectives, and therefore it is critical that these measurements are reported at all levels to see if the objectives are met. It helps to identify corrective actions and promote continuous improvement.

One of the areas where MA contributes, according to MA1 is in providing information for managerial decision-making and in controlling activities specifically by providing variances. Furthermore, management accountants contribute detailed information on performance variances to both the front-line employees and management to take corrective action.

HR1 explained that what all the HR strategies ultimately boil down to is an effective, efficient, productive mill and making a profit. Therefore, it is important to understand the cost elements. This is where MA plays a role: 'At this mill there is a real focus on cost control and therefore MA provides much more meaningful financial information that people can look at and say, okay, I know what my cost elements are and understand the cost drivers, and now I can begin to exercise some control over them.' HR1 commented on the importance of the contribution from MA in providing operational control activities, as it not only provides evaluation on improvement activities but is also very helpful for motivating employees to see the improved results or areas for improvement.

6.5 Summary

Considering all the areas of emphasis set by the corporate executives, and the HR strategies that are followed, there are basically four key areas that this mill is concentrating on: (1) work systems improvement – empowering, flexibility and total quality management; (2) leadership training; (3) safety; and (4) diversity. HR2 pointed out the two key areas of HR strategies: 'I think as the Vice President of Human Resources it is really satisfying for me to see as I look at our five business strategies that include *empowering* people, and that is one of the five core strategies of the company as well as *total quality management*. These strategies directly impact on people in the company.' Regarding the concept of making the company do its business by total quality: 'We are doing more than just making better products. We are safer and more productive. Since 1991, we have reduced the number of reportable accidents by 55 per cent. Meanwhile, our facilities report less downtime and improved production levels. Because of these successes, we are challenging ourselves to identify further improvements in our work systems.'

HR2's comment with respect to empowering people is of working towards a common goal. With respect to leadership, according to HR2, it is critical that there is total support from the top executives, full commitment and strongly reinforced at the mill level for successful outcomes of the HR strategies. HR4 commented on how important their people are: 'We are a very highly technical mill, state of the art! One of the best in North America. Where we are going to have a lot of success is working with our people, and that's what we are right now! So, for us the competitive edge is, *having the best people*, diversity in the workforce, and that is how we want to become the best forest products company in the world.'

None of the above HR strategies has been planned or implemented without the participation of management accountants. Looking at the overall HR strategic process, management accountants have contributed in planning, analysing and measuring both financial and non-financial measurements, fully participated in decision-making, and provided information in the management control process (Figure 6.5).

Figure 6.5 summarises the MA contribution in relation to the HR strategic process. The basis of the HR strategies is initiated from corporate objectives linking to corporation vision. The senior management team has filtered out the HR strategies, for example, WSI, WLE and safety. These strategies are basically developed from the HR areas of emphasis based on corporate objectives. The strategies are realigned at the mill level to suit the needs of the operation. The objectives of these strategies are to gain competitive advantage, safety in the workplace, quality of service/product and profitability and to develop leadership.

In the HR strategic process described above, management accountants have played different roles and made a contribution to achieving strategic objectives. For example, at the strategic level a management accountant has played a role as a key member of the executive committee where the MA contribution was in developing the HR areas of emphasis.

At the mill level, a management accountant played a role as a member of the leadership team in developing HR strategies for the pulp mill. In this capacity, management accountants provided analytical information for making decisions, contributed in the planning process and helped in setting targets for these HR strategies. For example, management accountants provided information about financial resources available for leadership training for the first-line supervisors. Management accountants made suggestions for giving opportunities for employees to be flexible as part of the WSI strategy.

Figure 6.5 Management accounting contribution in human resource strategic process

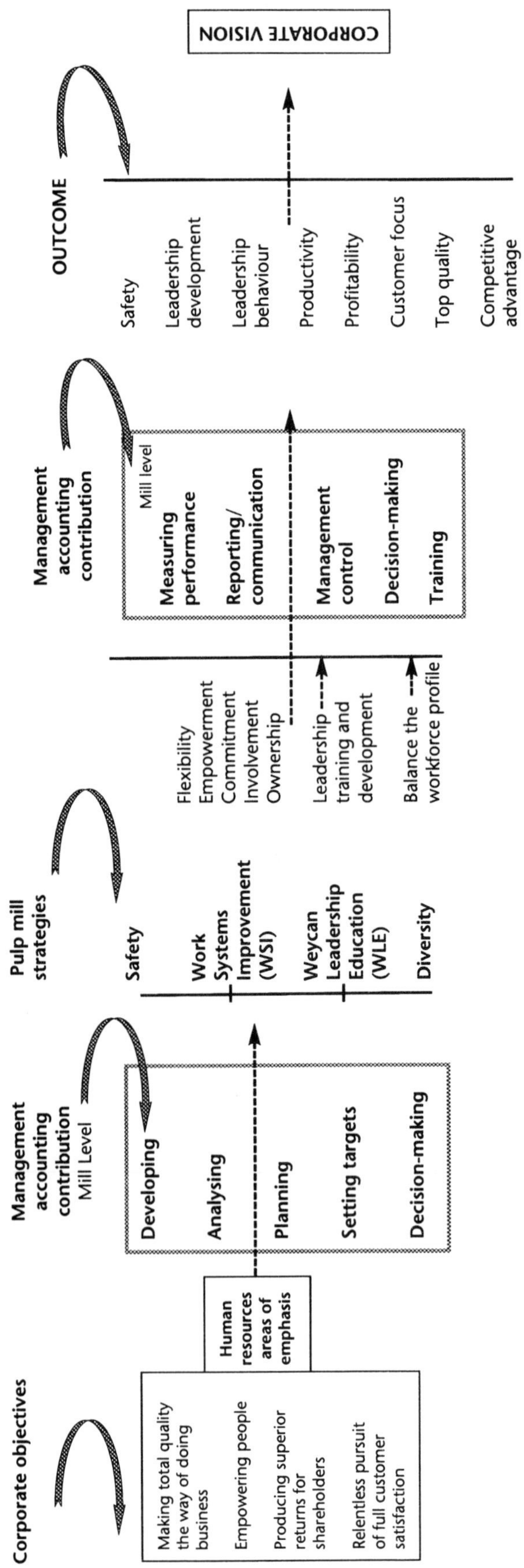

Management accounting played a key role in measuring both financial and non-financial performance. For example, compiling information on safety – number of accidents, number of safety seminars, issues on safety, procedures and policies – and providing information on monthly financial performance, including RONA. The monthly reporting package prepared by MA is first presented to the leadership team. This is where management accountants played a key role in discussing performance and provided suggestions for management control where and if necessary. These monthly reports are also communicated to all the staff members, including mill workers. In this case, management accountants acted as business partners and played a role as facilitator and business consultant.

Further, managers provided their views on the future role of MA. HR3 commented, 'I would like to see the Financial Manager do less work, I think we would be more advantaged by the Financial Manager working on the system rather than in the system. The role has changed, we want the Financial Manager to be a better business person rather than just a number-cruncher which is a past history done and over with.' He further explained how management accountants can contribute at the operational level where day-to-day critical operational decisions are made: 'To become a better business person, you have to get out and find out what people on the plant floor need. Find out what they do, what kind of decisions they make, what current information do they use to make those decisions, what information can you provide them to make better decisions. Once you get to that point than you can provide them with the information they understand how it all fits together, in order to make better decisions.' His final comments were, 'You got to be there with them in order to understand what they do and how they do it'.

The views of US2 on the future role of management accountants are as follows: 'I think in many aspects they play a valuable role. I think, where they could probably play a bigger role is in the presentation of information as opposed to just strictly raw data and they can play a very valuable role interpreting where the opportunities lie.' He further commented that financial people are leaders to support the areas of the business in achieving the mill objectives: 'I think one of the ways I have seen it really effectively addressed is by having cross-departmental teams including a finance manager.'

With respect to the future role of management accountants, US1 responded, 'I think they could be more involved in our day-to-day work. That would be a big benefit to all of us at the operational level.' US4 explained:

> The future role of MA is to provide more graphical information, trends over time, more analysis of the data, moving average and the data that is kind of tailored toward the operational side, those are the things that probably could help in day-to-day decision-making.

7

Conclusions

7.1 Introduction

The pivotal issues addressed in this research project are:

- the current role of MA in relation to SHRM;
- managers' views on the future role of MA in relation to SHRM.

In particular, the project sought insights into the information provided by MA within the context of the SHRM process, involving planning, analysing, formulating, implementing, setting targets, measuring and reporting performance.

Today, organisations face volatile challenges, and to survive and prosper they need to adapt to change quickly and effectively. SHRM is one way to change (Ezzamel et al., 1996). The role of MA is becoming more integrated and interdisciplinary (Bromwich and Bhimani, 1994), contributing information to tackle ever-changing challenges. Armstrong (1989, 1995) pointed out that there is a role for MA to support HRM activities. To gain an understanding of the process and techniques used with respect to the current role of MA in relation to strategic HRM, four in-depth case studies were undertaken.

7.2 Case studies

7.2.1 Key human resource strategies

The most common HR strategy highlighted in all cases is training and development. This includes leadership training and development, flexibility, work systems improvements, career development and teamwork training. It seems that companies are developing a valued workforce to improve organisational competitiveness and growth by providing training and development. Training and development is also one of the key components of HR strategy identified in the questionnaire surveys. Another component of the HR strategy is leadership. The evidence suggests that organisations have realised that to implement their HR strategies effectively, they must have appropriate leadership. Gupta and Govindarajan (1984) point out that without effective leadership it is unlikely that an organisation will realise the benefits of its selected strategy. Leadership training programmes are designed for managers and supervisors at all levels. Besides training and development and leadership training, the focus is also on health and safety. Organisations are becoming increasingly safety-conscious (e.g. Cases 3 and 4). The findings from the case studies reveal that management accountants have a role in analysing the above HR strategies by providing cost–benefit analyses for decision-making. An important aspect of the development of HR strategies is integration between MA and HRM. At one research site (Case 4), a management accountant played the role of facilitator during the leadership training sessions.

7.2.2 Management accounting contribution and strategic planning

Management accountants played a role in relation to the SHRM process in providing information in the HR strategic planning process. In all four cases, strategic guidelines and procedures are developed and derived from the organisational overall objectives and mission. The most common goals for all four case studies are:

- growing profitable volume;
- achieving business efficiency;
- creating the environment to add value to gain competitive advantage.

The concept of the development of HR strategies linking to corporate objectives is consistent with the findings from the questionnaire surveys and current HRM literature which emphasise the importance of strategy in the management of an organisation and the desirability of linking HR strategies with business strategies (Fombrun et al., 1984; Guest, 1987). Bratton (1994) also commented on a strategic component in defining strategic HRM where human resource activities need to be integrated with the corporate strategy to meet an organisation's objectives.

This research study establishes that the role of MA includes being involved in HR planning and strategic decisions (such as reducing the number of temporary employees and increasing the number of permanent employees to improve customer service).

The process of strategic planning and business planning is a team effort from different areas within the division, including a key role played by management accountants. This study clearly identified different aspects of the contribution by management accountants in different domains of the HR strategies and also at different levels of the organisation.

7.2.3 Analysis and decision-making

The case studies show that management accountants play a role in analysing HR strategies for strategic decision-making. The analytical contribution by management accountants is provided at a strategic level and also at a business planning level. Management accountants contribute and compile information for the planning and development of HR strategies. The strategy development and formulation process involves identifying strategic alternatives. These alternatives are developed in the light of the strengths, weaknesses, opportunities and threats facing the organisation, its mission and its strategic goals. Further, these strategic alternatives focus on improving organisational performance.

The management accountant as a member of the executive committee played a key role in contributing and developing the strategic alternatives, providing analytical information at the critical time of the strategic process. Simmonds (1981) used the term 'strategic management accounting' for the expanded role of management accounting in providing analysis in the development and monitoring of the strategy of the business that would assist strategic decision-making. In Case 2, one of the priorities is to push for decentralisation where the strategic planning process is an integrative approach. One role of management accountants is to provide information to develop strategies at Board level, to analyse and help implement strategies at divisional level and contribute to the decision-making process, such as decisions whether to work overtime or hire agency employees.

7.2 4 Measuring performance, reporting and communicating

Performance measurement involves monitoring the organisation's progress towards fulfilling its mission and achieving its strategic goals and plans. The findings illustrate that there is a contribution from management accountants in measuring HR performance (financial and non-financial), reporting and communicating. For example, management accountants are involved in preparing performance reports, compiling, monitoring, analysing and presenting the performance and providing suggestions for improvements if necessary. Armstrong (1995) points out that the outcomes of the HR strategies should be in a language that is meaningful to the Board for decision-making, and management accountants play a role in contributing measures that are critical in strategic decision-making.

Cases 1, 2 and 4 provided divisional reporting showing key performance indicators prepared at the divisional level, compiled by the management accounting group with information fed from all levels. These reports show both financial and non-financial indicators. One of the research sites (Case 3) recently went through a major change of information system where management accountants played a key role in the development of the new system to provide effective, efficient and more meaningful reporting. In Case 4, management accountants contribute information for benchmarking comparisons, including HR. The benchmarking indicators are a very critical part of the information used in making decisions.

One role of the management accountant is as a consultant, providing valuable information, communicating in a language that is understood by the users and helping managers to improve their performance. Management accountants provide information about the costs and effectiveness of the salary scheme and the training programme. Another role for management accountants is to provide analytical information in decision-making at the strategic level, planning, measuring performance, both financial and non-financial, and reporting and communicating at both corporate and divisional levels. The role of the management accountant is as a support and team player and consultant, in improving performance in all four cases. The major difference is in Case 3, the logistics business, where the contribution by management accountants is different at different sites, depending on the site and the type of business.

To summarise the above discussion, the following list highlights the key points:

- HR strategies are linked to organisational mission/goals/objectives.
- One of the key HR strategies identified in all cases is *training and development,* including *leadership training.*
- The management accountant is usually a key member of the executive committee where high-level HR strategic decisions are made.
- Management accountants contribute to SHRM in different ways such as:
  - providing information for SHRM planning;
  - analysing HRM strategies;
  - providing information for HRM decision-making;
  - measuring HRM performance (financial and non-financial);
  - benchmarking;
  - reporting HRM performance.

7.3 Limitations

As in any case study research, the results are specific to a particular site. A second limitation results from conscious or unconscious bias in the interviewers' interaction with respondents. In addition, case study information may be biased by the researchers' closeness to the situation. One of the criticisms is the researchers' bias in the collection and analysis of data. Furthermore, approximately two weeks were spent at each site and this is a limited period of time.

The above limitations have been partly overcome by drawing on multiple sources of data from four different case studies. Multiple methods and multiple sources of data help to limit the threats to validity and reliability and subjective bias (McKinnon, 1988; Bomoma, 1985). Nevertheless, this research project does have the above limitations.

7.4 Concluding comments

Among successful organisations, effective HR strategies have now become a distinguishing factor. In these four case studies, the organisations have concentrated on providing training and development, including leadership training, within a safe working environment to create a highly committed, competent and customer-oriented workforce.

In developing and shaping these HR strategies, the study reveals that MA plays a critical role at various stages of the SHRM process by contributing information and critical analysis in decision-making, planning, setting targets, measuring performance (both financial and non-financial), reporting and communicating at all levels. Therefore, there is a strategic role for management accountants – an integrating, supporting and consulting role with the management accountants as team players. However, the management accountant needs to understand the operations of the business, including the HR side of the business, to be able to work with the HR community and to communicate in order to help achieve HR strategic goals and to make the organisational vision a reality.

Nevertheless, HR managers foresee scope for an even greater contribution from management accountants in the area of SHRM in the future, particularly as regards more information for developing and setting SHRM targets, SHRM decision-making and measuring HRM performance. HR managers would also prefer to see the management accountant in future having a wider business knowledge and being more of a business partner. However, the results of this research project show that management accountants can and do contribute to the SHRM process.

References

Anthony, R.N. (1989). Reminiscences about management accounting. *Journal of Management Accounting Research,* 1, Fall, pp. 1–20.

Armstrong, P. (1989). Limits and possibilities of HRM in an age of management accountancy. In *New Perspectives on Human Resource Management* (ed. Storey, J.) Routledge, pp. 154–66.

Armstrong, P. (1995). Accountancy and HRM. In *Human Resource Management: A Critical Text.* (Ed. Story, J.). Routledge, pp. 142–63.

Arthur, J.B. (1994). Effects of human resource systems on manufacturing performance and turnover. *Academy of Management Journal,* Vol. 37, No. 3, pp. 670–87.

Barney, J. (1991). Firm resources and sustained competitive advantage. *Journal of Management,* Vol. 17, pp. 99–120.

Berliner, C. and Brimson, J.A. (eds) (1988). *Cost Management for Today's Advanced Manufacturing: The CAM-I Conceptual Design.* Boston: Harvard Business School Press.

Birkett, W.P. (1995). Management accounting and knowledge management. *Management Accounting,* November.

Bomoma, V.T. (1985). Case research in marketing: opportunites, problems and a process. *Journal of Marketing Research,* Vol. 22, pp. 199–208.

Bratton, J. (1994). Human resource management in transition. In *Human Resource Management – Theory and Practice* (eds Bratton, J. and Gold, J.). New York: Macmillan Press Ltd, pp. 3–31.

Bromwich, M. and Bhimani, A. (1989). Challenge of change. *Management Accounting,* October, pp. 5–6.

Bromwich, M. and Bhimani, A. (1994). The strategic dimensions. In *Management Accounting: Pathways to Progress.* London: Chartered Institute of Management Accountants.

Caillouet, A. and Lapeyre, B. (1992). The importance of an accounting information system in the strategic management process. *SAM Advanced Management Journal,* Winter, pp. 21–4.

Clarke, P. (1995). The old and the new in management accounting. Management context of human resource strategy. In *Bottom-Line Results From Strategic Human Resource Planning* (eds Neihaus, R. and Price, K.). New York: Plenum Press, pp. 235–46.

Collier, P. and Gregory, A. (1995). 'Strategic management accounting: a UK hotel sector case study. *International Journal of Contemporary Hospitality Management,* Vol. 7, No. 1, pp. 16–21.

Dessler, G. (1997). *Human Resource Management.* Prentice-Hall: New Jersey.

Dyer, I. and Reeves T. (1995). Human resource strategies and firm performance: what do we know and where do we need to go? *International Journal of Human Resource Management*, Vol. 6, No. 3, pp. 302–325. September.

Ezzamel, M., Lilley, S., Wilkinson, A. and Willmott, H. (1995). Practices and practicalities in human resource management. *Human Resource Management Journal*, Vol. 6, No. 1, pp. 63–80.

Fombrun, C.J., Tichy, N.M. and Devanna, M.J. (1984). *Strategic Human Resource Management*. New York: Wiley.

Grady, M.W. (1991). Performance measurement: implementing strategy. *Management Accounting* (US), June, pp. 49–53.

Guest, D.E. (1987). Human resource management and industrial relations. *Journal of Management Studies*, Vol. 24, No. 5, pp. 503–21.

Guest, D.E. (1989). Human resource management: its implications for industrial relations and trade unions. In *New Perspectives on Human Resource Management* (ed. Story, J.). Routledge, pp. 41–55.

Guest, D.E. (1990). Human resource management and the American dream. *Journal of Management Studies*, Vol. 27, No.4, pp. 377–97.

Gupta, A.K. and Govindarajan, V. (1984). Business unit strategy, managerial characteristics, and business unit effectiveness at strategy implementation. *Academy of Management Journal*, March, pp. 24–41.

Hendry, C. and Pettigrew, A. (1986). The practice of strategic human resource management. *Personnel Review*, Vol. 15, No. 5, pp. 3–8.

Hendry, C. and Pettigrew, A. (1990). HRM: an agenda for the 1990s. *International Journal of Human Resource Management*, Vol. 1, No. 1, pp. 17–25.

Hiromoto, T. (1988). Another hidden edge – Japanese management accounting', *Harvard Business Review*, July/August, pp. 23–6.

Howes, P. (1997). Strategic human resource management: an Australian case study. *Human Resource Planning*, Vol. 16, No. 3, pp. 53–64.

Huselid, M.A. (1995). The impact of human resource management practices on turnover, productivity and corporate financial performance. *Academy of Management Journal*, Vol. 38, No. 3, pp. 635–72.

Ichniowski, C., Shaw, K. and Prennushi, G. (1995). The effects of human resource management practices on productivity. *NBER Working Paper* 5333, November 1995. Industrial Relations Centre, Queen's University (Current Issues Series).

Ittner, C.D. and Larcker, D.F. (1997). Quality strategy, strategic control systems and organizational performance. *Accounting Organizations and Society*, Vol. 22, No. 3/4, pp. 293–314.

Johnson, H.T. and Kaplan, R.A. (1987). *Relevance Lost: The Rise and Fall of Management Accounting*. Boston: Harvard Business School Press.

Kamoche, K. (1996). Strategic human resource management within a resource-capability view of the firm. *Journal of Management Studies*, Vol. 33, No. 2, pp. 213–33.

Kaplan, R.S. (1983). Measuring manufacturing performance: a new challenge for managerial accounting research. *The Accounting Review*, Vol. LVIII, No. 4, pp. 686–705.

Kaplan, R.S. (1984). Yesterday's accounting undermines production. *Harvard Business Review*, July-August, pp. 95–101.

Kaplan, R.S. (1988). One cost system isn't enough. *Harvard Business Review,* January–February, pp. 61–6.

Kochan, T. and Dyer, L. (1995). HRM: an American view. In *Human Resource Management: A Critical Text* (ed. Storey, J.). London: Routledge, pp. 332–51.

Kouhy, R. and Vedd, R. (2000). Performance measurement in strategic human resource management. *International Journal of Business Performance Management,* Issue 1, Vol. 2, No.1, pp. 137–156.

Lado, A.A. and Wilson, M.C. (1994). Human resource systems and sustained competitive advantage: a competency-based perspective. *Academy of Management Review,* Vol. 19, No. 4, pp. 699–727.

Lawler, E.E. (1992). *The Ultimate Advantage: Creating the High-Involvement Organization.* San Francisco: Josey-Bass.

Legge, K. (1995). What is human resource management? In *Human Resource Management, Rhetorics and Realities.* New York: Macmillan Press, pp. 225–263.

Lengnick-Hall, C.A. and Lengnick-Hall, M.L. (1988). Strategic human resources management: a review of the literature and a proposed typology. *Academy of Management Review,* Vol. 13, No. 3, pp. 454–70.

Merriam, S. (1988). *Case Study Research in Education: A Qualitative Approach.* San Francisco: Jossey-Bass.

Miles, R.E. and Snow, C.C. (1978). *Environmental Strategy and Organizational Development.* New York: McGraw-Hill.

Mintzberg, H. (1990). *The design school: reconsidering the basic premises of strategy.* New Jersey: Prentice Hall.

Mintzberg, H. and Waters, J.A. (1985). Of strategies, deliberate and emergent. *Strategic Management Journal,* Vol. 6, No. 2, pp. 257–72.

Pfeffer, J. (1994). *Competitive Advantage Through People: Unleashing the Power of the Workforce.* Boston: Harvard Business School Press.

Porter, M.E. (1985). *Competitive Advantage: Creating and Sustaining Superior Performance.* New York: Quorum Books.

Purcell, J. (1995). Corporate strategy and its link with human resource management strategy. In *Human Resource Management: A Critical Text* (ed. Storey, J.). Routledge, pp. 63–86.

Riahi-Belkaoui, A. (1992). *The New Foundations of Management Accounting.* New York: Quorum Books.

Roslender, R., Hart, S. and Ghosh, J. (1998). Strategic management accounting: refocusing the agenda. *Management Accounting (London),* Vol. 76, No. 11, December, pp. 44–6.

Schuler, R.S. and Jackson, S.E. (1987). Linking competitive strategies with human resource management practices. *The Academy of Management Executive,* Vol. 1, No. 3, pp. 207–19.

Schuler, R.S. and Macmillan, I.C. (1984). Gaining competitive advantage through human resource practices. *Human Resource Management,* Vol. 23, No. 3, Fall, pp. 241–55.

Shank, J.K. and Govindarajan, V. (1993). *Strategic Cost Management – The New Tool for Competitive Advantage*. New York: The Free Press.

Simmonds, K. (1981). Strategic management accounting. *Management Accounting*, April, pp. 26–9.

Simon, C. (1992). *The Role of the Accountant in Strategic Planning: A Model for the 1990's*. Aldershot, UK: Gower.

Simons, R. (1990). The role of management control systems in creating competitive advantage: new perspectives. *Accounting, Organizations and Society*, Vol. 15, No. 1/2, pp. 127–43.

Storey, J. (1987). Development in the management of human resources: an interim report. *Warwick Papers in Industrial Relations*, 17. IRRU School of Industrial and Business Studies, University of Warwick (November).

Strauss, A. and Corbin, J. (1990). *Basics of Qualitative Research: Grounded Theory Procedures and Techniques*. Newbury Park, CA: Sage.

Townley, B. (1995). *A Foucauldian Analysis of Human Resource Management: Reframing Human Resource Management*. Sage.

Truss, C., Gratton, L., Hope-Hailey, V., McGovern, P. and Stiles, P. (1997). Soft and hard models of human resource management: a reappraisal. *Journal of Management Studies*, Vol. 34, No. 1, pp. 53–73.

Vaughan, E. (1994). The trail between sense and sentiment: a reflection on the language of HRM. *Journal of General Management*, Vol. 19, No. 13, pp. 10–32.

Vilgoen, J. (1994). *Review of Strategic Management: Planning and Implementing Successful Corporate Strategies*, 2nd edn. Longman Business and Profession.

Ward, K. (1992). *Strategic Management Accounting*. Oxford: Butterworth-Heinemann.

Wright, P.M. and McMahan, G.E. (1992). Theoretical perspectives for strategic human resource management. *Journal of Management*, Vol. 18, No. 2, pp. 295–320.